HOW TO MAKE FROZEN YOGURT

56 Delicious Flavors You Can Make at Home

Nicole Weston

Storey Publishing

*The mission of Storey Publishing is to serve our customers by
publishing practical information that encourages
personal independence in harmony with the environment.*

Edited by Margaret Sutherland
Series design by Alethea Morrison
Art direction by Cynthia N. McFarland
Text production by Theresa Wiscovitch

Cover illustration by © Lisel Ashlock
Interior illustrations by © Holly Exley

Storey Publishing
210 MASS MoCA Way
North Adams, MA 01247
www.storey.com

Printed in the United States by McNaughton & Gunn, Inc.
10 9 8 7 6 5 4 3 2 1

Library of Congress Cataloging-in-Publication Data

Weston, Nicole.
 How to make frozen yogurt / by Nicole Weston.
    pages cm
  "A Storey basics title."
  Includes index.
  ISBN 978-1-61212-377-6 (pbk. : alk. paper)
  ISBN 978-1-61212-378-3 (ebook) 1. Frozen yogurt. I. Title.
TX795.W48 2014
641.3'71476—dc23
                2013040122

CONTENTS

FROZEN YOGURT RECIPES

Gourmet

Holiday

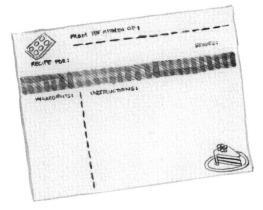

PART ONE

INTRODUCTION TO FROZEN YOGURT

As a kid on hot summer days in Southern California, I always looked forward to enjoying a cool treat after a long day at school. Sometimes I had an ice-cold soda or a smoothie, but the treat I loved most was frozen yogurt.

When frozen yogurt first became popular, it was a soft-serve substitute for ice cream. It was sweet and creamy, but it came in very few identifiable flavors and its main selling point was that it was a lower-fat, more healthful alternative to traditional ice cream. It was hugely popular when it became available in the early 1980s, but growth in the frozen yogurt market slowed after a few years because the yogurt itself was bland and more compelling as a vehicle for toppings like shredded coconut, yogurt chips, and rainbow sprinkles than as a unique treat.

Plain yogurt has a tart, tangy flavor that comes from the natural cultures that are used to turn ordinary milk into what we know as yogurt. Yogurt wasn't very popular when frozen yogurt was first introduced, except among the very health conscious, but as better-tasting, thicker yogurts grew in popularity, frozen yogurt also started to change — and to taste like yogurt. That signature yogurt tang became a hallmark of high-quality frozen yogurts made with premium ingredients. This new style of frozen yogurt launched a yogurt revolution, and it is now more popular than ever before.

The recipes that follow show you how to make frozen desserts at home with the tangy, fresh flavor of premium frozen yogurts.

HOW TO MAKE FROZEN YOGURT

FROZEN YOGURT IS A DESSERT made with yogurt as its base, but there is a big difference between yogurt that has been frozen and frozen yogurt. Yogurt that has been frozen is grainy and icy. It shatters instead of scooping and does not blend well with added ingredients.

Frozen yogurt should be creamy and smooth, and — like ice cream — it should be something that you can store in your freezer and scoop when you want to eat some. It's easy to make at home, and making your own frozen yogurt gives you complete control of the ingredients and flavors that will go into your desserts.

Frozen yogurt does present some challenges that ice cream does not.

Yogurt doesn't freeze well on its own because a major component of yogurt is whey, the watery part of milk. Whey freezes solid, just like water. So what happens when you freeze plain yogurt is it develops icy crystals and loses its texture — and the same thing can happen to homemade frozen yogurt. You end up with something that's a far cry from the creamy, smooth texture that you want in a frozen dessert.

Commercially made frozen yogurts often have stabilizers added to enhance their texture, and commercial machines can infuse enough extra air into the base to keep the frozen yogurt soft. Home ice cream makers aren't as powerful as commercial machines, but there are a few things you can do to ensure that your frozen yogurt tastes delicious and stays scoopable even after sitting in the freezer for a few days.

The first trick is to minimize the amount of whey in your frozen yogurt base by using thick, Greek-style yogurt, which already has a lot of the whey strained out of it. This thicker yogurt will be less likely to form large ice crystals when frozen. The second trick is to use full-fat yogurt and dairy, since the little bit of extra fat will help give your frozen yogurt additional creaminess. The small amount of fat will also help prevent the yogurt from freezing too hard. Finally, the most important thing you can do to achieve a pleasing, scoopable texture is to infuse extra air into your yogurt mixture before churning. I call this the Meringue Method, because I use an easy-to-make meringue to aerate the base and help ensure a deliciously smooth finished product every time.

The Meringue Method

The Meringue Method for making frozen yogurt involves using a cooked meringue, also known as an Italian meringue, to incorporate extra air into the frozen yogurt base before the churning phase. Meringue is a mixture of egg whites and sugar that is beaten until stiff and foamy. Most meringues are made with raw eggs and then incorporated into recipes that call for cooking the meringue before serving. The Italian meringue uses a different technique to produce meringue that is completely cooked and safe to eat without any additional cooking or baking; it is an ideal addition to frozen yogurt. The meringue is very easy to make and makes a big difference in the creaminess of the finished yogurt.

To make a cooked meringue, you first beat room temperature egg whites until they're foamy. Then you slowly stream boiling sugar into the egg whites while beating them until soft peaks form. The egg whites in the finished meringue are completely cooked; you can fold them into any yogurt mixture without additional cooking.

Another advantage of the Meringue Method is that the melted sweetener for the recipe is easily incorporated into the yogurt. Many recipes call for long periods of strong stirring to dissolve granulated sugar into the yogurt. So, though it may seem complicated at first, it takes only a few minutes to make the meringue, and the results are well worth the effort.

1) Beat egg whites to soft peaks.

2) Pour boiled sugar into egg whites.

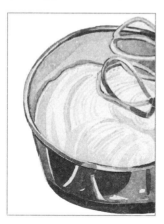

3) Beat to a glossy, finished meringue.

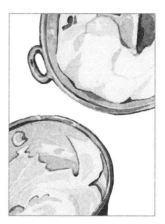

4) Fold meringue into yogurt mixture.

Making Frozen Yogurt with an Ice Cream Maker

Most of the recipes in this book call for using an ice cream maker to churn your frozen yogurt base into actual frozen yogurt. There is a wide variety of ice cream makers on the market. They come in many sizes and in a range of prices, so you are sure to find something that will suit your needs. An ice cream maker will give you the best results and allow you to make frozen yogurt much more quickly than doing it by hand.

The purpose of an ice cream maker is to chill an ice cream or frozen yogurt base mixture quickly while adding air to it. Rapid chilling reduces the number and size of ice crystals in the finished product, so it will be smooth and creamy. Adding air to the mixture softens it, making it easy to scoop when frozen. That added air also makes frozen desserts taste better, since slight aeration allows the frozen mixture to melt smoothly and evenly on your tongue.

THE THREE MAIN TYPES

The Hand Churn Ice Cream Maker is the most basic kind. With this type of gadget, you add your own ice and salt to one chamber and your ice cream or frozen yogurt base to the other, and then you shake or stir while the base thickens up. This maker is very inexpensive and produces softer ice creams, but it works and it gives you a real workout as you churn up each batch.

The Canister Ice Cream Maker is the most common type. This model has a thick-walled canister: you freeze it in advance, and then you simply pour your base into the frozen canister and churn away. Some canister models require you to hand churn your ice cream or frozen yogurt, but most are small electric appliances that will do the work for you. Some stand mixers even offer canister attachments that will temporarily turn the mixer into an ice cream maker. The only drawback with this appliance is that you have to do some advance planning, making sure to put the canister in the freezer about 24 hours before you want to make your frozen yogurt.

The Compressor Ice Cream Maker is the most expensive type. The internal compressor starts to freeze your base as soon as you turn the appliance on. You don't have to prefreeze anything, and you don't even need to chill your dessert base before adding it to the machine, although doing so speeds up the freezing process. The advantage of this type of ice cream maker is that the machine is always ready to go and is capable of making multiple batches, one right after another, with no waiting time. This sort of pricey machine may not suit the occasional ice cream maker, but if you love to make ice cream or find that you are often serving a crowd, you can get a lot of use out of one of these.

hand churn
ice cream maker

canister
ice cream maker

compressor
ice cream maker

Making Frozen Yogurt without an Ice Cream Maker

Ice cream makers turn the process of creating frozen yogurt into a job that's quick and easy, but it is possible to make frozen yogurt without an ice cream maker. To do this, simply make the yogurt base of your choice and pour it into a large baking dish. Place the baking dish in the freezer and come back and give the mixture a thorough stir with a fork after 15 to 20 minutes. This breaks up any large ice crystals that may have formed during the freezing. Check back every 15 to 20 minutes and repeat the stirring process until the base has become thick and is mostly frozen. At this point, you can stir in any flavorings the recipe calls for and then serve your frozen yogurt or transfer it to another container for longer storage.

Frozen yogurt made without an ice cream maker will still have great flavor, but it may have some chunks of ice in it that batches made in an ice cream maker won't have. It might also freeze harder if you store it long term and require some extra defrosting time before you can scoop and serve it.

FAQS

Q What is Greek-style yogurt?

A Greek-style yogurt is plain yogurt that has been strained to remove excess whey, resulting in a yogurt that is much thicker and creamier in consistency than ordinary yogurt. Authentic Greek-style yogurt does not get its texture from the addition of gelatin or stabilizers. Greek-style yogurt is available in many flavors, but the distinctive tangy flavor of plain is best for making flavorful frozen yogurt.

You can easily turn ordinary yogurt into Greek-style yogurt by straining it through a very fine sieve or cheesecloth for a few hours to remove most of the whey.

Q Do I need to use Greek-style yogurt?

A The excess whey — the watery part of milk — that is in regular yogurt will turn to ice when you use it in frozen yogurt. The frozen yogurt will still taste good straight out of the ice cream maker, but it will be a harder and icier frozen yogurt than one made with Greek-style yogurt.

Q What brand of yogurt should I use?

A You can use any brand of yogurt; choose one that you like. You can even use homemade yogurt. Since you'll be adding flavorings and sweeteners, you should choose plain yogurt, not flavored yogurt, for these recipes.

Q Can I use nonfat or low-fat yogurt?

A Yes, both nonfat and low-fat yogurt will turn out very tasty frozen yogurts and can be used in any of the recipes in this book. Full-fat yogurt will produce a creamier, richer-tasting product, which is why I recommend it for most frozen yogurts.

Q Can I reduce the sugar?

A You can reduce the sugar, but your results will not be the same as with the original recipe. The frozen yogurt may be too hard and icy or may taste too tart if you reduce the sugar. Sugar has two important functions in frozen yogurt recipes. It helps the frozen yogurt to remain creamy and smooth, rather than icy, and it also ensures just the right amount of sweetness in the finished dessert. The base for frozen yogurt will taste sweeter before it has been frozen, and you may find that your finished product is not sweet enough if you reduce the sugar in the initial recipe, even though the unfrozen base seems sweet.

Q Does the Meringue Method really cook the egg whites?

A Yes, the boiling sugar is hot enough to cook the egg whites and make them completely safe to eat.

Q Can I use processed egg whites instead of from separated eggs?

A Processed egg whites are not ideal for making meringues. Though these egg whites are convenient, the pasteurization process toughens some of the proteins in the eggs and prevents the whites from whipping up into fluffy meringues. It could take up to twice as long to beat processed egg whites to soft peaks, and they won't be as fluffy as fresh egg whites will be.

Q Do I need an ice cream maker?

A I've included instructions for making frozen yogurt without an ice cream maker, but you will generally get better results using an ice cream maker. An ice cream maker speeds up the freezing process and reduces the number of large ice crystals, resulting in a creamier finished product.

Q Can I eat my frozen yogurt straight out of the ice cream maker?

A Yes, you can eat it as soon as it is done churning. It will have a soft-serve consistency as this stage; after a couple of hours in the freezer, it will set up completely.

Q Does the frozen yogurt need to soften before scooping?

A Like many premium ice creams, frozen yogurt will need a few minutes to soften before scooping if you want to get a big, perfect scoop. Freezer temperatures vary, but you can expect to be able to scoop it after a few minutes at room temperature. If you are storing your frozen yogurt in a very deep container, it may need a few extra minutes. Running your ice cream scoop under hot water before scooping will help it to slide through your frozen yogurt more easily.

HOW TO MAKE YOUR OWN YOGURT

GREAT FROZEN YOGURT STARTS WITH delicious yogurt, so you should always choose a brand whose flavor you like. Alternatively, you can make your own yogurt and use it as a base for your frozen yogurt creations.

Yogurt is easy to make at home and yogurt fans might find that they like their homemade version better than anything available at the grocery store. You need to start with some bacteria to get the yogurt process going. You can either purchase yogurt cultures from a specialty catalog or use a small amount of a favorite brand of yogurt that contains live, active Lactobacillus acidophilus cultures, the bacteria that turn milk into yogurt. If you are going to use store-bought yogurt as a starter, read the label carefully to ensure that it contains live cultures, or your homemade yogurt will not thicken up properly. The best yogurts to use will have very short ingredient lists and will not include stabilizers or thickeners, such as gelatin or cornstarch. Once you have made a batch of your own yogurt, you can reserve a small portion of it to act as a starter for your next batch.

Yogurt cultures are temperature sensitive, so you will want to use an instant-read thermometer when you're making yogurt. You may also want to invest in a yogurt maker, which makes the process just about foolproof and also allows you to easily portion your yogurt into small containers for serving. If you decide you want to make your own yogurt on a regular basis, a yogurt maker is a great investment that you will repay you for a long time to come.

Nevertheless, even without a yogurt maker, you can make yogurt at home — you'll just need to keep a closer eye on your mixture as it develops to make sure it stays in a good temperature range for the cultures.

Plain Yogurt

  4 cups (1 quart) whole milk
  ¼ cup plain yogurt with live, active yogurt cultures,
     at room temperature

1. Bring the milk to a simmer in a large saucepan.

2. Remove the pan from the heat just before the milk boils.
   Cool the milk to 110°F, using a thermometer to check the
   temperature.

3. Place the yogurt in a small bowl. When the milk has cooled
   to 110°F, add about 1 cup of the milk to the yogurt and whisk
   until the yogurt is completely incorporated. Pour the yogurt
   mixture back into the milk and whisk to combine.

   If using a yogurt maker: Divide the milk mixture into the containers
   of your yogurt maker and process according to the manufacturer's
   directions. Yogurt should be refrigerated after processing.

   If not using a yogurt maker: Transfer the milk mixture to a large,
   clean jar or container with an airtight lid and close the lid tightly.

   Place the jar in a very warm place and allow the yogurt to
thicken undisturbed for about 10 hours. Ideally, the jar should be
maintained at approximately 110 to 115°F as the yogurt thickens.
High shelves in warm rooms are good locations, and you can also
create a warm environment for your yogurt by setting your oven to
"warm." Check your warm place with a thermometer to see that it
is in the right temperature range before you place your jar there. If
you're using your oven, you may find when you do your temperature
check that cracking the door slightly results in the right temperature range.

Makes about 4 cups

Greek-Style Yogurt

Greek-style yogurt can easily be made at home by straining some of the excess whey from a batch of plain yogurt. You can strain store-bought plain yogurt or homemade yogurt, and both will give you a wonderfully thick product to serve as the base of your frozen yogurts. You can use whole-milk, low-fat, or nonfat yogurt for this process. Different brands have different consistencies, so the draining time may vary slightly from batch to batch. Choose a high-quality yogurt that doesn't have additives or stabilizers in it.

You will need a very fine strainer to drain the whey without losing any of the yogurt. A strainer lined with cheesecloth is ideal because you can handle any quantity of yogurt, but the coffee filters that fit in your home coffeemaker (2- to 6-cup size) work well if you don't mind working in batches. You can use a very fine unlined strainer if you don't have either cheesecloth or coffee filters on hand.

4 cups (1 quart) plain yogurt

1. Line a large strainer with 2 layers of cheesecloth, making sure that some of the cloth hangs over the sides of the strainer.

2. Place the strainer over a large bowl and fill with yogurt. Cover yogurt with extra cheesecloth and squeeze gently. Allow to sit for 1 to 2 hours at room temperature or up to 12 hours in the refrigerator. Excess whey will drain into the bowl.

(continued on next page)

3. When the yogurt remaining in the strainer is thick and creamy, transfer it to another container for storage in the refrigerator or use in frozen yogurt recipes. Discard the excess whey.

Makes about 3 cups

PART TWO

FROZEN YOGURT RECIPES

CLASSICS

Tangy and Tart

This tart, tangy frozen yogurt delivers all the flavor of plain yogurt in a slightly sweeter — and colder — package. This is a staple of every yogurt shop out there, and it is the most basic frozen yogurt you can make at home.

- ¼ cup water
- ⅔ cup sugar
- 2 large egg whites, room temperature
- 2 cups plain Greek-style yogurt, cold
- 1 teaspoon vanilla extract (optional)

1. Combine the water and sugar in a small saucepan and bring to a boil, without stirring, over medium-high heat. When the sugar mixture comes to a full boil, continue to boil for 1 minute.

2. While the sugar boils, beat the egg whites to soft peaks in a large, clean bowl. When the sugar is ready, continue beating the eggs at low speed and very slowly stream in the hot sugar mixture. When all the sugar has been incorporated, turn the mixer to high and beat until the meringue is glossy and has cooled almost down to room temperature, 2 to 3 minutes. (See The Meringue Method, page 4.)

3. Put the yogurt and vanilla, if using, in a large bowl and whisk until smooth. Fold in the meringue.

4. Pour the yogurt mixture into an ice cream maker and freeze according to the manufacturer's directions.

5. Transfer to a freezer-safe container and chill in the freezer for 2 to 3 hours to allow the yogurt to completely set.

Makes 1¼ to 1½ quarts

Vanilla Bean

Vanilla beans have a wonderfully floral flavor and aroma that you don't find anywhere else, even with vanilla extract. Using real vanilla beans to flavor this frozen yogurt makes the vanilla the star.

¼ cup water

⅔ cup sugar

1 vanilla bean

2 large egg whites, room temperature

2 cups plain Greek-style yogurt, cold

(continued on next page)

1. Combine the water and sugar in a small saucepan. Split the vanilla bean lengthwise and scrape the seeds out using the back of a knife. Stir the seeds into the sugar mixture. Bring to a boil, without stirring, over medium-high heat. When the sugar mixture comes to a full boil, continue to boil for 1 minute.

2. While the sugar boils, beat the egg whites to soft peaks in a large, clean bowl. When the sugar is ready, continue beating the eggs at low speed and very slowly stream in the hot sugar mixture. When all the sugar has been incorporated, turn the mixer to high and beat until the meringue is glossy and has cooled almost down to room temperature, 2 to 3 minutes. (See The Meringue Method, page 4.)

3. Put the yogurt in a large bowl and whisk until smooth. Fold in the meringue.

4. Pour the yogurt mixture into an ice cream maker and freeze according to the manufacturer's directions.

5. Transfer to a freezer-safe container and chill in the freezer for 2 to 3 hours to allow the yogurt to completely set.

Makes 1¼ to 1½ quarts

Chocolate

Chocolate frozen yogurt, along with tart and vanilla, are shop staples. This version has a mild chocolate flavor that will satisfy chocolate cravings without being too rich. You'll still be able to taste some of the tanginess of the yogurt behind the cocoa, too.

½ cup whole milk

¼ cup unsweetened cocoa powder

¼ cup water

⅔ cup sugar

2 large egg whites, room temperature

2 cups plain Greek-style yogurt, cold

1 teaspoon vanilla extract

1. Bring the milk to a simmer in a small saucepan. Add the cocoa powder and stir to dissolve. Set aside to cool slightly.

2. Combine the water and sugar in a small saucepan and bring to a boil, without stirring, over medium-high heat. When the sugar mixture comes to a full boil, continue to boil for 1 minute.

3. While the sugar boils, beat the egg whites to soft peaks in a large, clean bowl. When the sugar is ready, continue beating the eggs at low speed and very slowly stream in the hot sugar mixture. When all the sugar has been incorporated, turn the mixer to high and beat until the meringue is glossy and has cooled almost down to room temperature, 2 to 3 minutes. (See The Meringue Method, page 4.)

(continued on next page)

4. Whisk together the yogurt, vanilla, and cocoa mixture in a large bowl until smooth. Fold in the meringue.

5. Pour the yogurt mixture into an ice cream maker and freeze according to the manufacturer's directions.

6. Transfer to a freezer-safe container and chill in the freezer for 2 to 3 hours to allow the yogurt to completely set.

Makes 1¼ to 1½ quarts

Dark Chocolate

The dark chocolate flavor of this frozen yogurt will be first choice for chocoholics. The chocolate is melted and incorporated into the warm meringue before being folded into the yogurt. The rich but not-too-sweet dark chocolate flavor of this special treat will feel very indulgent. Choose a high-quality chocolate for best results.

- ¼ cup water
- ⅔ cup sugar
- 2 large egg whites, room temperature
- 4 ounces dark chocolate (60–70% cacao), coarsely chopped
- 2 cups plain Greek-style yogurt, cold
- 2 teaspoons vanilla extract

1. Combine the water and sugar in a small saucepan and bring to a boil, without stirring, over medium-high heat. When the sugar mixture comes to a full boil, continue to boil for 1 minute.

2. While the sugar boils, beat the egg whites to soft peaks in a large, clean bowl. When the sugar is ready, continue beating the eggs at low speed and very slowly stream in the hot sugar mixture. When all the sugar has been incorporated, turn the mixer to high and beat until the meringue is glossy and has cooled almost down to room temperature, 2 to 3 minutes. (See The Meringue Method, page 4.)

3. In a small microwave-safe bowl, melt the chocolate in the microwave, heating it on high power in 30- to 45-second intervals, stirring frequently until the chocolate is smooth. With the mixer on low speed, blend the melted chocolate into the meringue.

4. Whisk together the yogurt and vanilla in a large bowl until smooth. Fold in the meringue.

5. Pour the yogurt mixture into an ice cream maker and freeze according to the manufacturer's directions.

6. Transfer to a freezer-safe container and chill in the freezer for 2 to 3 hours to allow the yogurt to completely set.

Makes 1¼ to 1½ quarts

Coffee

Coffee delivers just as much of a pick-me-up in frozen yogurt as it does in a latte. A regular cup of coffee won't give frozen yogurt enough flavor, however, so this recipe uses instant coffee or espresso powder to give it a strong coffee punch.

½ cup whole milk

2 tablespoons instant coffee or espresso powder

¼ cup water

⅔ cup sugar

2 large egg whites, room temperature

2 cups plain Greek-style yogurt, cold

1 teaspoon vanilla extract

1. Bring the milk to a simmer in a small saucepan. Add the coffee and stir to dissolve. Set aside to cool slightly.

2. Combine the water and sugar in a small saucepan and bring to a boil, without stirring, over medium-high heat. When the sugar mixture comes to a full boil, continue to boil for 1 minute.

3. While the sugar boils, beat the egg whites to soft peaks in a large, clean bowl. When the sugar is ready, continue beating the eggs at low speed and very slowly stream in the hot sugar mixture. When all the sugar has been incorporated, turn the mixer to high and beat until the meringue is glossy and has cooled almost down to room temperature, 2 to 3 minutes. (See The Meringue Method, page 4.)

4. Whisk together the yogurt, vanilla, and coffee mixture in a large bowl until smooth. Fold in the meringue.

5. Pour the yogurt mixture into an ice cream maker and freeze according to the manufacturer's directions.

6. Transfer to a freezer-safe container and chill in the freezer for 2 to 3 hours to allow the yogurt to completely set.

Makes 1¼ to 1½ quarts

FRUITS

Double Blueberry

Blueberries are a popular topping over plain yogurt at breakfast time, especially during the summer when blueberries are at their peak. In this frozen yogurt the berry is showcased as both a rich sauce and in its whole form. If you don't have time to make the sauce, you can use a high-quality blueberry jam in this recipe instead.

- ¼ cup water
- ⅔ cup sugar
- 2 large egg whites, room temperature
- 2 cups plain Greek-style yogurt, cold
- ⅔ cup Easy Blueberry Sauce (recipe follows)
- 2 teaspoons vanilla extract
- ¾ cup fresh blueberries

1. Combine the water and sugar in a small saucepan and bring to a boil, without stirring, over medium-high heat. When the sugar mixture comes to a full boil, continue to boil for 1 minute.

2. While the sugar boils, beat the egg whites to soft peaks in a large, clean bowl. When the sugar is ready, continue beating the eggs at low speed and very slowly stream in the hot sugar mixture. When all the sugar has been incorporated, turn the mixer to high and beat until the meringue is glossy and has cooled almost down to room temperature, 2 to 3 minutes. (See The Meringue Method, page 4.)

3. Whisk together the yogurt, blueberry sauce, and vanilla in a large bowl until smooth. Fold in the meringue.

4. Pour the yogurt mixture into an ice cream maker and freeze according to the manufacturer's directions.

5. When the yogurt has finished churning and is still soft, transfer to a large bowl. Fold in the fresh blueberries until evenly distributed.

6. Transfer to a freezer-safe container and chill in the freezer for 2 to 3 hours to allow the yogurt to completely set.

Makes 1¼ to 1½ quarts

Easy Blueberry Sauce

You can double this recipe and use the extra sauce as a topping with this frozen yogurt or other flavors.

> 1 cup fresh or frozen blueberries
> ¼ cup water
> 1 tablespoon fresh lemon juice
> ⅓ cup sugar

(continued on next page)

Combine the blueberries, water, lemon juice, and sugar in a small saucepan and bring to a boil over medium-high heat. Cook, stirring, until the sugar has dissolved and the fruit begins to break down. Reduce the heat to medium and continue cooking until the sauce has reduced slightly, 3 to 5 minutes. Remove from the heat and cool completely before using. Sauce can be stored in an airtight container in the refrigerator for 3 to 5 days.

Makes about ⅓ cup

Key Lime

Key lime pie is a dessert that translates very well to frozen yogurt because it already has a smooth, creamy filling. Adding sweetened condensed milk tempers the tanginess of the lime juice and will give your frozen yogurt that familiar flavor of the classic pie. If you can't find Key limes, you can substitute regular limes for both the lime juice and the lime zest. You will get the best flavor using fresh lime juice, rather than juice from concentrate.

- ¼ cup water
- ½ cup sugar
- 2 large egg whites, room temperature
- 2 cups plain Greek-style yogurt, cold
- ½ cup sweetened condensed milk
- ⅓ cup fresh Key lime juice (4–5 Key limes)
- 1 teaspoon Key lime zest

1. Combine the water and sugar in a small saucepan and bring to a boil, without stirring, over medium-high heat. When the sugar mixture comes to a full boil, continue to boil for 1 minute.

2. While the sugar boils, beat the egg whites to soft peaks in a large, clean bowl. When the sugar is ready, continue beating the eggs at low speed and very slowly stream in the hot sugar mixture. When all the sugar has been incorporated, turn the mixer to high and beat until the meringue is glossy and has cooled almost down to room temperature, 2 to 3 minutes. (See The Meringue Method, page 4.)

3. Whisk together the yogurt, condensed milk, lime juice and zest in a large bowl until smooth. Fold in the meringue.

4. Pour the yogurt mixture into an ice cream maker and freeze according to the manufacturer's directions.

5. Transfer to a freezer-safe container and chill in the freezer for 2 to 3 hours to allow the yogurt to completely set.

Makes 1¼ to 1½ quarts

Mango

Creamy, luscious mangoes are often combined with yogurt in fruit smoothies, but they make an even better frozen yogurt. The small amount of lemon juice in this recipe brings out the natural sweetness of the mangoes.

    1–2 ripe mangoes
    ¼ cup fresh lemon juice
    ⅔ cup sugar
    2 large egg whites, room temperature
    2 cups plain Greek-style yogurt, cold

(continued on next page)

1. Peel and roughly chop the mangoes, and then purée in a food processor until very smooth. You should have about 1 cup of mango purée.

2. Combine the lemon juice and sugar in a small saucepan and bring to a boil, without stirring, over medium-high heat. When the sugar mixture comes to a full boil, continue to boil for 1 minute.

3. While the sugar boils, beat the egg whites to soft peaks in a large, clean bowl. When the sugar is ready, continue beating the eggs at low speed and very slowly stream in the hot sugar mixture. When all the sugar has been incorporated, turn the mixer to high and beat until the meringue is glossy and has cooled almost down to room temperature, 2 to 3 minutes. (See The Meringue Method, page 4.)

4. Whisk together the yogurt and mango purée in a large bowl until smooth. Fold in the meringue.

5. Pour the yogurt mixture into an ice cream maker and freeze according to the manufacturer's directions.

6. Transfer to a freezer-safe container and chill in the freezer for 2 to 3 hours to allow the yogurt to completely set.

Makes 1¼ to 1½ quarts

Lemon Meringue

Homemade lemon curd gives this frozen yogurt the same bright lemon flavor that you look forward to in a lemon meringue pie. The difference here is that the meringue and the lemon curd are blended to create a zesty frozen treat! The lemon curd needs to be made in advance, but you can double the recipe and store the extra lemon curd to enjoy later with toast or scones for breakfast.

⅓ cup fresh lemon juice

⅔ cup sugar

2 large egg whites, room temperature

2 cups plain Greek-style yogurt, cold

⅔ cup Lemon Curd (recipe follows)

1. Combine the lemon juice and sugar in a small saucepan and bring to a boil, without stirring, over medium-high heat. When the sugar mixture comes to a full boil, continue to boil for 1 minute.

2. While the sugar boils, beat the egg whites to soft peaks in a large, clean bowl. When the sugar is ready, continue beating the eggs at low speed and very slowly stream in the hot sugar mixture. When all the sugar has been incorporated, turn the mixer to high and beat until the meringue is glossy and has cooled almost down to room temperature, 2 to 3 minutes. (See The Meringue Method, page 4.)

3. Whisk together the yogurt and lemon curd in a large bowl until smooth. Fold in the meringue.

(continued on next page)

4. Pour the yogurt mixture into an ice cream maker and freeze according to the manufacturer's directions.

5. Transfer to a freezer-safe container and chill in the freezer for 2 to 3 hours to allow the yogurt to completely set.

Makes 1¼ to 1½ quarts

Homemade Lemon Curd

⅓ cup strained fresh lemon juice

⅓ cup sugar

1 large egg, room temperature

2 tablespoons butter, cold and cut into 4 pieces

1. Combine the lemon juice and sugar in a small saucepan and bring to a simmer over medium heat until the sugar has completely dissolved.

2. Lightly beat the egg in a medium bowl. Whisking constantly, very slowly stream in the hot lemon syrup.

3. When all the syrup has been incorporated, pour the mixture into the pan and cook over medium-low heat, stirring constantly, until the curd just starts to thicken and bubble at the edges. Remove from the heat and stir in the butter one piece at a time until all the butter has melted into the curd.

4. Transfer the curd to a small bowl and cover with plastic wrap, pressing it down onto the surface of the curd. Cool completely before using. Leftover curd can be stored in the refrigerator for up to 1 month. The lemon curd will thicken as it cools.

Makes about ⅔ cup

Fresh Strawberry

Strawberry is a perennial favorite at any ice cream shop, but nothing beats frozen strawberry yogurt made at home with fresh berries. The fresh berries shine through in this frozen yogurt and add a bright pink color. To make the strawberry purée, simply remove the tops from your berries and purée the fruit in a food processor or blender until perfectly smooth.

10–12	ounces fresh strawberries
¼	cup water
⅔	cup sugar
2	large egg whites, room temperature
2	cups plain Greek-style yogurt, cold
½	teaspoon vanilla extract

1. Wash and hull the strawberries, and then purée in a food processor until very smooth. You should have about 1 cup of strawberry purée.

2. Combine the water and sugar in a small saucepan and bring to a boil, without stirring, over medium-high heat. When the sugar mixture comes to a full boil, continue to boil for 1 minute.

3. While the sugar boils, beat the egg whites to soft peaks in a large, clean bowl. When the sugar is ready, continue beating the eggs at low speed and very slowly stream in the hot sugar

(continued on next page)

mixture. When all the sugar has been incorporated, turn the mixer to high and beat until the meringue is glossy and has cooled almost down to room temperature, 2 to 3 minutes. (See The Meringue Method, page 4.)

4. Whisk together the yogurt, strawberry purée, and vanilla in a large bowl until smooth. Fold in the meringue.

5. Pour the yogurt mixture into an ice cream maker and freeze according to the manufacturer's directions.

6. Transfer to a freezer-safe container and chill in the freezer for 2 to 3 hours to allow the yogurt to completely set.

Makes 1¼ to 1½ quarts

Black Cherry Vanilla

Sweet black cherries and vanilla create an unforgettable combination in ice cream and are just as delicious in frozen yogurt. For an extra flavor accent, add some shaved chocolate or chocolate chips to the recipe.

    1 cup fresh or frozen black cherries
    ½ cup sugar
    ½ vanilla bean
    ¼ cup water
    ½ cup sugar
    2 large egg whites, room temperature
    2 cups plain Greek-style yogurt, cold
    1 teaspoon vanilla extract

1. Coarsely chop the cherries, removing any pits. Combine the cherries and sugar in a medium saucepan. Split the vanilla

bean lengthwise and scrape the seeds out using the back of a knife. Stir the seeds into the cherry mixture. Bring the cherries to a boil over medium-high heat and cook, stirring occasionally, until the sugar has dissolved. Reduce the heat to medium and continue cooking until the syrup has thickened and reduced to 1 cup. Remove from the heat and set aside to cool.

2. Combine the water and sugar in a small saucepan and bring to a boil, without stirring, over medium-high heat. When the sugar mixture comes to a full boil, continue to boil for 1 minute.

3. While the sugar boils, beat the egg whites to soft peaks in a large, clean bowl. When the sugar is ready, continue beating the eggs at low speed and very slowly stream in the hot sugar mixture. When all the sugar has been incorporated, turn the mixer to high and beat until the meringue is glossy and has cooled almost down to room temperature, 2 to 3 minutes. (See The Meringue Method, page 4.)

4. Whisk together the yogurt and vanilla in a large bowl until smooth. Fold in the meringue.

5. Pour the yogurt mixture into an ice cream maker and freeze according to the manufacturer's directions.

6. When the yogurt has finished churning and is still soft, transfer to a large bowl. Fold in the cherry syrup until completely incorporated.

7. Transfer to a freezer-safe container and chill in the freezer for 2 to 3 hours to allow the yogurt to completely set.

Makes 1¼ to 1½ quarts

Rich Toasted Coconut

The richness and extra coconut flavor of this frozen yogurt come from the coconut cream, the thick, almost pastelike liquid that comes from pressing fresh coconut meat and removing some of the water. Besides the wonderful coconut flavor and richness of this recipe, the coconut cream makes for an especially smooth frozen yogurt.

- ¼ cup water
- ⅔ cup sugar
- 2 large egg whites, room temperature
- 2 cups plain Greek-style yogurt, cold
- ⅔ cup coconut cream
- 1 teaspoon vanilla extract
- 1 cup toasted coconut (instructions follow), very finely chopped

1. Combine the water and sugar in a small saucepan and bring to a boil, without stirring, over medium-high heat. When the sugar mixture comes to a full boil, continue to boil for 1 minute.

2. While the sugar boils, beat the egg whites to soft peaks in a large, clean bowl. When the sugar is ready, continue beating the eggs at low speed and very slowly stream in the hot sugar mixture. When all the sugar has been incorporated, turn the mixer to high and beat until the meringue is glossy and has cooled almost down to room temperature, 2 to 3 minutes. (See The Meringue Method, page 4.)

3. Whisk together the yogurt, coconut cream, and vanilla in a large bowl until very smooth. Fold in the meringue and stir in the coconut.

4. Pour the yogurt mixture into an ice cream maker and freeze according to the manufacturer's directions.

5. Transfer to a freezer-safe container and chill in the freezer for 2 to 3 hours to allow the yogurt to completely set.

Makes 1¼ to 1½ quarts

Toasted Coconut

1 cup sweetened, shredded coconut

To toast the coconut in the oven, spread the shredded coconut in a thin layer on a baking sheet. Bake at 300°F for about 20 minutes, until the coconut is mostly golden brown, stirring every 5 minutes to make sure that the coconut browns evenly.

To toast the coconut on the stove top, spread the shredded coconut into a skillet and cook over medium heat, stirring frequently, until the coconut is mostly golden brown, 5 to 8 minutes.

Cool completely before using or storing in an airtight container.

Makes 1 cup

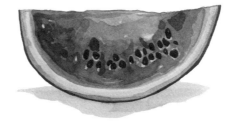

Watermelon

Ice-cold watermelon is as refreshing as it gets on a hot summer day. To allow the subtle flavor of the watermelon to stand up to the yogurt, this recipe uses slightly less yogurt and a little more watermelon. Watermelon used as is will give the yogurt a somewhat coarse texture, so it's best to purée it and strain out the pulp for a refreshing yet smooth and creamy frozen yogurt.

  2 cups diced watermelon
¼ cup fresh lime juice
¼ cup water
⅔ cup sugar
  2 large egg whites, room temperature
  2 cups plain Greek-style yogurt, cold
  1 tablespoon melon liqueur (optional)

1. Purée the watermelon with the lime juice in a food processor or blender. Press through a medium-fine sieve into a small bowl and set aside. Discard the solids. You should have about 1½ cups. If you do not have enough juice, repeat this step

with more watermelon. If you have more juice, the excess can be discarded or added to a cocktail or smoothie.

2. Combine the water and sugar in a small saucepan and bring to a boil, without stirring, over medium-high heat. When the sugar mixture comes to a full boil, continue to boil for 1 minute.

3. While the sugar boils, beat the egg whites to soft peaks in a large, clean bowl. When the sugar is ready, continue beating the eggs at low speed and very slowly stream in the hot sugar mixture. When all the sugar has been incorporated, turn the mixer to high and beat until the meringue is glossy and has cooled almost down to room temperature, 2 to 3 minutes. (See The Meringue Method, page 4.)

4. Whisk together the yogurt, watermelon juice, and liqueur, if using, in a large bowl until smooth. Fold in the meringue.

5. Pour the yogurt mixture into an ice cream maker and freeze according to the manufacturer's directions.

6. Transfer to a freezer-safe container and chill in the freezer for 2 to 3 hours to allow the yogurt to completely set.

Makes 1¼ to 1½ quarts

Apple Pie

A scoop of ice cream is the perfect accompaniment to a slice of apple pie, and those same flavors are a sure hit in frozen yogurt – especially when the apple pie is added directly to the yogurt! Homemade apple pie filling is easy to make and delivers all the flavor of apple pie right into your yogurt. You can add some of the syrup to your yogurt base, but hold off on the apple pieces until after the churning because they will be too large for most ice cream makers to handle. The filling also makes a wonderful topping for this frozen yogurt: its recipe can be doubled to give you the extra.

- ¼ cup water
- ½ cup sugar
- 2 large egg whites, room temperature
- 2 cups plain Greek-style yogurt, cold
- 1 teaspoon vanilla extract
- 1½ cups Apple Pie Filling (recipe follows)

1. Combine the water and sugar in a small saucepan and bring to a boil, without stirring, over medium-high heat. When the sugar mixture comes to a full boil, continue to boil for 1 minute.

2. While the sugar boils, beat the egg whites to soft peaks in a large, clean bowl. When the sugar is ready, continue beating the eggs at low speed and very slowly stream in the hot sugar mixture. When all the sugar has been incorporated, turn the mixer to high and beat until the meringue is glossy and has cooled almost down to room temperature, 2 to 3 minutes. (See The Meringue Method, page 4.)

3. Whisk together the yogurt and vanilla in a large bowl until smooth. Fold in the meringue.

4. Pour the yogurt mixture into an ice cream maker and freeze according to the manufacturer's directions.

5. When the yogurt has finished churning and is still soft, transfer to a large bowl. Fold in the filling until completely incorporated.

6. Transfer to a freezer-safe container and chill in the freezer for 2 to 3 hours to allow the yogurt to completely set.

Makes 1¼ to 1½ quarts

Apple Pie Filling

> 1½ cups diced peeled apples
> ¼ cup granulated sugar
> ½ cup firmly packed brown sugar
> 1 teaspoon ground cinnamon
> ½ teaspoon ground ginger
> ½ teaspoon ground allspice
> ½ teaspoon vanilla extract
> 1 tablespoon cornstarch
> 1 tablespoon butter

Combine the apples, granulated sugar, brown sugar, cinnamon, ginger, allspice, vanilla, cornstarch, and butter in a medium saucepan. Bring the apple mixture to a boil over medium-high heat and cook, stirring occasionally, until the sugar has dissolved. Reduce the heat to medium and continue cooking until the apples are tender and the syrup has thickened, 10 to 15 minutes. Remove from the heat and cool completely before using.

Makes about 1½ cups

Roasted Banana and Salted Caramel

Roasting bananas in the oven intensifies their sweetness and breaks down any of the starch that is left in the fruit, making them even creamier. Here, the creamy sweetness is paired with a salted caramel sauce that has just enough edge to satisfy a salty-sweet craving. You can use a store-bought caramel sauce or the homemade version below.

3	medium bananas, unpeeled
¼	cup water
⅓	cup sugar
2	large egg whites, room temperature
2	cups plain Greek-style yogurt, cold
1	teaspoon vanilla extract
¼ plus ⅓	cup Salted Caramel Sauce (recipe follows)

1. Preheat the oven to 375°F. Place the bananas on a foil-lined baking sheet and roast until black and very tender, about 25 minutes. Set aside to cool completely.

2. Combine the water and sugar in a small saucepan and bring to a boil, without stirring, over medium-high heat. When the sugar mixture comes to a full boil, continue to boil for 1 minute.

3. While the sugar boils, beat the egg whites to soft peaks in a large, clean bowl. When the sugar is ready, continue beating the eggs at low speed and very slowly stream in the hot sugar mixture. When all the sugar has been incorporated, turn the mixer to high and beat until the meringue is glossy and has cooled almost down to room temperature, 2 to 3 minutes. (See The Meringue Method, page 4.)

4. Peel the roasted bananas and mash the flesh in a large bowl until very smooth. Add the yogurt, vanilla, and ¼ cup of the caramel sauce and whisk until smooth. Fold in the meringue.

5. Pour the yogurt mixture into an ice cream maker and freeze according to the manufacturer's directions.

6. When the yogurt has finished churning and is still soft, transfer to a large bowl. Drizzle in the remaining ⅓ cup caramel sauce while folding the ice cream to create a swirl.

7. Transfer to a freezer-safe container and chill in the freezer for 2 to 3 hours to allow the yogurt to completely set.

Makes 1¼ to 1½ quarts

Salted Caramel Sauce

    ½ cup sugar
    ⅓ cup corn syrup
    ¼ cup water
      Salt
    ¾ cup heavy cream
    1 teaspoon vanilla extract
    1 teaspoon coarse or kosher salt

1. Combine the sugar, corn syrup, water, and a small pinch of salt in a medium saucepan and cook over medium heat, stirring with a spatula, until the sugar has dissolved.

2. When the sugar has dissolved, bring the mixture to a boil, without stirring, over medium-high heat and cook until it turns a dark caramel color, 7 to 10 minutes.

(continued on next page)

3. Combine the cream and vanilla in a small bowl or measuring cup. When the caramel has reached the desired color, remove from the heat and quickly add the cream and vanilla. The mixture will bubble vigorously and may separate. Return to the heat and cook, stirring constantly, over medium-high heat until the mixture is smooth and creamy and the ingredients are completely blended, 2 to 3 minutes. Remove from the heat and cool completely in another container before using. Caramel may be made one day in advance and should be stored in an airtight container at room temperature.

Makes about 1 cup

SUGAR AND SPICES

Ginger and Cardamom

Spicy ginger and bright, floral cardamom come together with a hint of lemon and vanilla in this frozen yogurt. The combination of ginger and cardamom is enough to give any dish an exotic twist, and this is no exception. Be sure to strain out the fibrous ginger before putting the base to churn.

- ½ cup whole milk
- 2 tablespoons freshly grated ginger
- 3 whole cardamom pods, crushed
- 1 teaspoon lemon zest
- ¼ cup water
- ⅔ cup sugar
- 2 large egg whites, room temperature
- 2 cups plain Greek-style yogurt, cold
- 1 teaspoon vanilla extract

(continued on next page)

1. Combine the milk, ginger, cardamom, and lemon zest in a small saucepan and bring to a simmer. Remove from the heat and allow the spices to steep for 30 minutes.

2. Strain the spice-infused milk into a clean bowl and set aside. Discard the solids.

3. Combine the water and sugar in a small saucepan and bring to a boil, without stirring, over medium-high heat. When the sugar mixture comes to a full boil, continue to boil for 1 minute.

4. While the sugar boils, beat the egg whites to soft peaks in a large, clean bowl. When the sugar is ready, continue beating the eggs at low speed and very slowly stream in the hot sugar mixture. When all the sugar has been incorporated, turn the mixer to high and beat until the meringue is glossy and has cooled almost down to room temperature, 2 to 3 minutes. (See The Meringue Method, page 4.)

5. Whisk together the yogurt, vanilla, and spice-infused milk in a large bowl until smooth. Fold in the meringue.

6. Pour the yogurt mixture into an ice cream maker and freeze according to the manufacturer's directions.

7. Transfer to a freezer-safe container and chill in the freezer for 2 to 3 hours to allow the yogurt to completely set.

Makes 1¼ to 1½ quarts

Chai Spice

Chai tea is made with a wide variety of spices and is known for its complex flavor. This frozen yogurt is infused with some of those distinctive flavors that make the tea so delicious. Ground rather than crushed spices make the process easier.

- 1 cup whole milk
- 1½ teaspoons ground cinnamon
- 1 teaspoon ground ginger
- ½ teaspoon ground allspice
- ½ teaspoon ground cardamom
- ¼ teaspoon ground cloves
- 2 teaspoons vanilla extract
- ¼ teaspoon almond extract
- ¼ cup water
- ⅔ cup sugar
- 2 large egg whites, room temperature
- 2 cups plain Greek-style yogurt, cold

1. Bring the milk to a simmer in a small saucepan over medium heat. Combine the cinnamon, ginger, allspice, cardamom, and cloves with 1 teaspoon of the vanilla and the almond extract in a small heatproof bowl. Pour the hot milk over the spice mixture and stir well. Let steep undisturbed for 1 hour. (Most of the spices will sink to the bottom.)

2. Combine the water and sugar in a small saucepan and bring to a boil, without stirring, over medium-high heat. When the sugar mixture comes to a full boil, continue to boil for 1 minute.

(continued on next page)

3. While the sugar boils, beat the egg whites to soft peaks in a large, clean bowl. When the sugar is ready, continue beating the eggs at low speed and very slowly stream in the hot sugar mixture. When all the sugar has been incorporated, turn the mixer to high and beat until the meringue is glossy and has cooled almost down to room temperature, 2 to 3 minutes. (See The Meringue Method, page 4.)

4. Whisk together in a large bowl until smooth the yogurt, the remaining 1 teaspoon vanilla, and spice-infused milk, being careful to get any of the spice mixture at the bottom of the bowl. Fold in the meringue.

5. Pour the yogurt mixture into an ice cream maker and freeze according to the manufacturer's directions.

6. Transfer to a freezer-safe container and chill in the freezer for 2 to 3 hours to allow the yogurt to completely set.

Makes 1¼ to 1½ quarts

Earl Grey

Earl Grey tea is comfort in a cup for many tea lovers. Its distinctive flavor comes from the peel of the bergamot orange, complemented here by the addition of a fragrant vanilla bean. You can use vanilla extract instead, but the combination of the vanilla bean and Earl Grey tea is like a match made in heaven.

⅔ cup whole milk
6 Earl Grey tea bags
1 vanilla bean
¼ cup water

⅔ cup sugar

2 large egg whites, room temperature

2 cups plain Greek-style yogurt, cold

1. Combine the milk and tea bags in a small saucepan. Split the vanilla bean lengthwise and scrape the seeds out using the back of a knife. Add the seeds to the milk and bring the mixture to a simmer over medium heat. Turn off the heat and allow the tea bags to steep for 15 minutes. Remove the tea bags and allow the mixture to cool to room temperature.

2. Combine the water and sugar in a small saucepan and bring to a boil, without stirring, over medium-high heat. When the sugar mixture comes to a full boil, continue to boil for 1 minute.

3. While the sugar boils, beat the egg whites to soft peaks in a large, clean bowl. When the sugar is ready, continue beating the eggs at low speed and very slowly stream in the hot sugar mixture. When all the sugar has been incorporated, turn the mixer to high and beat until the meringue is glossy and has cooled almost down to room temperature, 2 to 3 minutes. (See The Meringue Method, page 4.)

4. Whisk together the yogurt and tea-infused milk until smooth. Fold in the meringue.

5. Pour the yogurt mixture into an ice cream maker and freeze according to the manufacturer's directions.

6. Transfer to a freezer-safe container and chill in the freezer for 2 to 3 hours to allow the yogurt to completely set.

Makes 1¼ to 1½ quarts

Matcha Green Tea

Matcha is a brightly colored, finely milled green tea powder that is also popular in many culinary applications because of its bold color and distinctive, slightly bitter flavor. It can be found at Asian markets and is also available at many specialty grocers and tea shops. The tanginess of the Greek yogurt is a good match for the flavor of the matcha, and there is just enough sweetness to create the perfect balance.

½ cup whole milk

3 tablespoons matcha powder

¼ cup water

⅔ cup sugar

2 large egg whites, room temperature

2 cups plain Greek-style yogurt, cold

1 teaspoon vanilla extract

1. Bring the milk to a simmer in a small saucepan. Add the matcha powder and stir to dissolve. Set aside and allow to cool to room temperature.

2. Combine the water and sugar in a small saucepan and bring to a boil, without stirring, over medium-high heat. When the sugar mixture comes to a full boil, continue to boil for 1 minute.

3. While the sugar boils, beat the egg whites to soft peaks in a large, clean bowl. When the sugar is ready, continue beating the eggs at low speed and very slowly stream in the hot sugar mixture. When all the sugar has been incorporated, turn the mixer to high and beat until the meringue is glossy and has

cooled almost down to room temperature, 2 to 3 minutes.
(See The Meringue Method, page 4.)

4. Whisk together the yogurt, vanilla, and matcha-infused milk
   in a large bowl until smooth. Fold in the meringue.

5. Pour the yogurt mixture into an ice cream maker and freeze
   according to the manufacturer's directions.

6. Transfer to a freezer-safe container and chill in the freezer for
   2 to 3 hours to allow the yogurt to completely set.

Makes 1¼ to 1½ quarts

Cookie Butter

*Biscoff spread has the creamy consistency of peanut butter but is made
from buttery brown-sugar and spice-flavored cookies. It is thick, sweet,
and downright addictive — especially when it's mixed into frozen
yogurt, where it gives the plain yogurt a rich texture and brown sugar
sweetness. The addition of crushed Biscoff cookies packs in more of
that irresistible flavor and a crunch for contrast.*

    ¼ cup water
    ½ cup sugar

(ingredients continued on next page)

2 large egg whites, room temperature

2 cups plain Greek-style yogurt, cold

¾ cup Biscoff spread

1 teaspoon vanilla extract

¾ cup crushed Biscoff cookies

1. Combine the water and sugar in a small saucepan and bring to a boil, without stirring, over medium-high heat. When the sugar mixture comes to a full boil, continue to boil for 1 minute.

2. While the sugar boils, beat the egg whites to soft peaks in a large, clean bowl. When the sugar is ready, continue beating the eggs at low speed and very slowly stream in the hot sugar mixture. When all the sugar has been incorporated, turn the mixer to high and beat until the meringue is glossy and has cooled almost down to room temperature, 2 to 3 minutes. (See The Meringue Method, page 4.)

3. Beat together the yogurt, Biscoff spread, and vanilla in a large bowl until smooth. Fold in the meringue.

4. Pour the yogurt mixture into an ice cream maker and freeze according to the manufacturer's directions.

5. When the yogurt has finished churning and is still soft, transfer to a large bowl. Stir in the crushed Biscoff cookies until evenly distributed.

6. Transfer to a freezer-safe container and chill in the freezer for 2 to 3 hours to allow the yogurt to completely set.

Makes 1¼ to 1½ quarts

Maple Syrup

The rich, sweet flavor of maple syrup stands out in this frozen yogurt. Be sure to choose Grade B maple syrup, which is darker in color and will give you the richest maple syrup flavor. Don't be tempted to substitute inexpensive pancake syrup, a product that's made with maple-flavored corn syrup and not the real thing.

- ¼ cup water
- ½ cup sugar
- 2 large egg whites, room temperature
- 2 cups plain Greek-style yogurt, cold
- ½ teaspoon vanilla extract
- ½ cup maple syrup

1. Combine the water and sugar in a small saucepan and bring to a boil, without stirring, over medium-high heat. When the sugar mixture comes to a full boil, continue to boil for 1 minute.

(continued on next page)

2. While the sugar boils, beat the egg whites to soft peaks in a large, clean bowl. When the sugar is ready, continue beating the eggs at low speed and very slowly stream in the hot sugar mixture. When all the sugar has been incorporated, turn the mixer to high and beat until the meringue is glossy and has cooled almost down to room temperature, 2 to 3 minutes. (See The Meringue Method, page 4.)

3. Whisk together the yogurt, vanilla, and maple syrup in a large bowl until smooth. Fold in the meringue.

4. Pour the yogurt mixture into an ice cream maker and freeze according to the manufacturer's directions.

5. Transfer to a freezer-safe container and chill in the freezer for 2 to 3 hours to allow the yogurt to completely set.

Makes 1¼ to 1½ quarts

Honey

Honey is the most popular way to top off a bowl of Greek-style yogurt, since the intense natural sweetness of the honey contrasts well with the tanginess of the yogurt. Honey is sweet, but that sweetness is what will keep you coming back for seconds.

¼ cup water

½ cup sugar

2 large egg whites, room temperature

2 cups plain Greek-style yogurt, cold

½ cup honey

2 teaspoons vanilla extract

1. Combine the water and sugar in a small saucepan and bring to a boil, without stirring, over medium-high heat. When the sugar mixture comes to a full boil, continue to boil for 1 minute.

2. While the sugar boils, beat the egg whites to soft peaks in a large, clean bowl. When the sugar is ready, continue beating the eggs at low speed and very slowly stream in the hot sugar mixture. When all the sugar has been incorporated, turn the mixer to high and beat until the meringue is glossy and has cooled almost down to room temperature, 2 to 3 minutes. (See The Meringue Method, page 4.)

3. Whisk together the yogurt, honey, and vanilla in a large bowl until smooth. Fold in the meringue.

4. Pour the yogurt mixture into an ice cream maker and freeze according to the manufacturer's directions.

5. Transfer to a freezer-safe container and chill in the freezer for 2 to 3 hours to allow the yogurt to completely set.

Makes 1¼ to 1½ quarts

CHOCOLATE AND NUTS

Cookies 'n' Cream

Cream-filled chocolate sandwich cookies, such as Oreos, have such a great flavor that they are often featured in other sweets — like cookies 'n' cream ice cream, a perennial favorite. These delectable cookies work their magic in frozen yogurt just as successfully.

- ¼ cup water
- ⅔ cup sugar
- 2 large egg whites, room temperature
- 2½ cups plain Greek-style yogurt, cold
- 2 teaspoons vanilla extract
- ⅔ cup *finely* chopped chocolate sandwich cookies, such as Oreos
- ⅔ cup *coarsely* chopped chocolate sandwich cookies, such as Oreos

1. Combine the water and sugar in a small saucepan and bring to a boil, without stirring, over medium-high heat. When the sugar mixture comes to a full boil, continue to boil for 1 minute.

2. While the sugar boils, beat the egg whites to soft peaks in a large, clean bowl. When the sugar is ready, continue beating the eggs at low speed and very slowly stream in the hot sugar mixture. When all the sugar has been incorporated, turn the mixer to high and beat until the meringue is glossy and has cooled almost down to room temperature, 2 to 3 minutes. (See The Meringue Method, page 4.)

3. Whisk together the yogurt, vanilla, and the finely chopped cookies in a large bowl until smooth. Fold in the meringue.

4. Pour the yogurt mixture into an ice cream maker and freeze according to the manufacturer's directions.

5. When the yogurt has finished churning and is still soft, transfer to a large bowl. Fold in the coarsely chopped cookies until evenly distributed.

6. Transfer to a freezer-safe container and chill in the freezer for 2 to 3 hours to allow the yogurt to completely set.

Makes 1¼ to 1½ quarts

Chocolate Chip

Chocolate chips are a classic flavor addition to just about any frozen dessert. Store-bought chocolate chips tend to be large and become too hard when frozen, but making your own chips nicely takes care of this. Drizzle melted chocolate into your freshly made frozen yogurt, and you'll get crisp, easy-to-eat chocolate chips!

¼ cup water

⅔ cup sugar

2 large egg whites, room temperature

2 cups plain Greek-style yogurt, cold

2 teaspoons vanilla extract

4 ounces semisweet or dark chocolate, melted

1. Combine the water and sugar in a small saucepan and bring to a boil, without stirring, over medium-high heat. When the sugar mixture comes to a full boil, continue to boil for 1 minute.

2. While the sugar boils, beat the egg whites to soft peaks in a large, clean bowl. When the sugar is ready, continue beating the eggs at low speed and very slowly stream in the hot sugar mixture. When all the sugar has been incorporated, turn the mixer to high and beat until the meringue is glossy and has cooled almost down to room temperature, 2 to 3 minutes. (See The Meringue Method, page 4.)

3. Whisk together the yogurt and vanilla in a large bowl until smooth. Fold in the meringue.

4. Pour the yogurt mixture into an ice cream maker and freeze according to the manufacturer's directions.

5. When the yogurt has finished churning and is still soft, transfer to a large bowl. Drizzle the melted chocolate over the frozen yogurt while stirring the yogurt with a spatula to create small chocolate "chips" in the yogurt. Stir until all the chocolate has been used and the chips are evenly distributed.

6. Transfer to a freezer-safe container and chill in the freezer for 2 to 3 hours to allow the yogurt to completely set.

Makes 1¼ to 1½ quarts

Rocky Road

Chocolate goes well with so many flavors, but few combinations are as beloved as Rocky Road. Chocolate frozen yogurt handles the toasted walnuts and fluffy marshmallows just as well as ice cream, and the slight tang of the yogurt brings out the sweet marshmallows just a little more than usual.

> ½ cup whole milk
> ¼ cup unsweetened cocoa powder
> ¼ cup water
> ⅔ cup sugar
> 2 large egg whites, room temperature
> 2 cups plain Greek-style yogurt, cold
> 1 teaspoon vanilla extract
> ½ cup mini marshmallows
> ½ cup coarsely chopped walnuts

(continued on next page)

1. Bring the milk to a simmer in a small saucepan. Add the cocoa powder and stir to dissolve. Set aside to cool slightly.

2. Combine the water and sugar in a small saucepan and bring to a boil, without stirring, over medium-high heat. When the sugar mixture comes to a full boil, continue to boil for 1 minute.

3. While the sugar boils, beat the egg whites to soft peaks in a large, clean bowl. When the sugar is ready, continue beating the eggs at low speed and very slowly stream in the hot sugar mixture. When all the sugar has been incorporated, turn the mixer to high and beat until the meringue is glossy and has cooled almost down to room temperature, 2 to 3 minutes. (See The Meringue Method, page 4.)

4. Whisk together the yogurt, vanilla, and cocoa mixture in a large bowl until smooth. Fold in the meringue.

5. Pour the yogurt mixture into an ice cream maker and freeze according to the manufacturer's directions.

6. When the yogurt has finished churning and is still soft, transfer to a large bowl. Fold in the marshmallows and walnuts until evenly distributed.

7. Transfer to a freezer-safe container and chill in the freezer for 2 to 3 hours to allow the yogurt to completely set.

Makes 1¼ to 1½ quarts

Chocolate Chip Cookie Dough

There is something irresistible about a buttery, sticky-sweet cookie dough, especially when it's surrounded by vanilla ice cream. This vanilla frozen yogurt might just be a better match for the cookie dough than ice cream. The homemade cookie dough has no eggs, so the chunks are perfectly safe to eat unbaked.

- ¼ cup water
- ⅔ cup sugar
- 2 large egg whites, room temperature
- 2 cups plain Greek-style yogurt, cold
- 2 teaspoons vanilla extract
- 1 batch Chocolate Chip Cookie Dough Chunks (recipe follows), about 1 cup

1. Combine the water and sugar in a small saucepan and bring to a boil, without stirring, over medium-high heat. When the sugar mixture comes to a full boil, continue to boil for 1 minute.

2. While the sugar boils, beat the egg whites to soft peaks in a large, clean bowl. When the sugar is ready, continue beating

(continued on next page)

the eggs at low speed and very slowly stream in the hot sugar mixture. When all the sugar has been incorporated, turn the mixer to high and beat until the meringue is glossy and has cooled almost down to room temperature, 2 to 3 minutes. (See The Meringue Method, page 4.)

3. Whisk together the yogurt and vanilla in a large bowl until smooth. Fold in the meringue.

4. Pour the yogurt mixture into an ice cream maker and freeze according to the manufacturer's directions.

5. When the yogurt has finished churning and is still soft, transfer to a large bowl. Fold in the cookie dough chunks until evenly distributed.

6. Transfer to a freezer-safe container and chill in the freezer for 2 to 3 hours to allow the yogurt to completely set.

Makes 1¼ to 1½ quarts

Chocolate Chip Cookie Dough Chunks

⅓ cup butter, room temperature
½ cup firmly packed brown sugar
½ teaspoon vanilla extract
¼ teaspoon salt
1 tablespoon whole milk
½ cup all-purpose flour
½ cup mini chocolate chips

1. Cream together the butter and sugar in a medium bowl. Add the vanilla, salt, and milk, and blend well. Add the flour

and mix until the dough comes together. Fold in the chocolate chips.

2. Roll the dough into almond-size balls. Store the cookie dough balls in the refrigerator in an airtight container until ready to use, or for up to 2 to 3 days. They do not need to be separated once shaped.

Makes about 1 cup

Mocha

You don't need to be a barista to know that mochas are popular, hot or cold. Chocolate and coffee are a natural combination, since the two flavors intensify each other. To accent the coffee, you can double the amount of instant coffee used in the base. To highlight the chocolate, mix in some chocolate chips after churning.

- ½ cup whole milk
- 1 tablespoon instant coffee or espresso powder
- 3 tablespoons unsweetened cocoa powder
- ¼ cup water
- ⅔ cup sugar
- 2 large egg whites, room temperature
- 2 cups plain Greek-style yogurt, cold
- 2 teaspoons vanilla extract

1. Bring the milk to a simmer in a small saucepan. Add the coffee and cocoa and stir to dissolve. Set aside to cool slightly.

(continued on next page)

2. Combine the water and sugar in a small saucepan and bring to a boil, without stirring, over medium-high heat. When the sugar mixture comes to a full boil, continue to boil for 1 minute.

3. While the sugar boils, beat the egg whites to soft peaks in a large, clean bowl. When the sugar is ready, continue beating the eggs at low speed and very slowly stream in the hot sugar mixture. When all the sugar has been incorporated, turn the mixer to high and beat until the meringue is glossy and has cooled almost down to room temperature, 2 to 3 minutes. (See The Meringue Method, page 4.)

4. Whisk together the yogurt, vanilla, and milk mixture in a large bowl until smooth. Fold in the meringue.

5. Pour the yogurt mixture into an ice cream maker and freeze according to the manufacturer's directions.

6. Transfer to a freezer-safe container and chill in the freezer for 2 to 3 hours to allow the yogurt to completely set.

Makes 1¼ to 1½ quarts

Chocolate Malted

A shake made with malted milk powder can take you right back to the days of the old-time soda fountain, and while the powder can be added to all kinds of drinks and baked treats, there is nothing more classic than a chocolate malted. That distinctive malty flavor seems to make the chocolate creamier and the whole thing even more addictive.

½ cup whole milk
⅓ cup malted milk powder

4 tablespoons unsweetened cocoa powder

¼ cup water

⅔ cup sugar

2 large egg whites, room temperature

2 cups plain Greek-style yogurt, cold

1 teaspoon vanilla extract

1. Bring the milk to a simmer in a small saucepan. Add the malted milk and cocoa and stir to dissolve. Set aside to cool slightly.

2. Combine the water and sugar in a small saucepan and bring to a boil, without stirring, over medium-high heat. When the sugar mixture comes to a full boil, continue to boil for 1 minute.

3. While the sugar boils, beat the egg whites to soft peaks in a large, clean bowl. When the sugar is ready, continue beating the eggs at low speed and very slowly stream in the hot sugar mixture. When all the sugar has been incorporated, turn the mixer to high and beat until the meringue is glossy and has cooled almost down to room temperature, 2 to 3 minutes. (See The Meringue Method, page 4.)

4. Whisk together the yogurt, vanilla, and cocoa mixture in a large bowl until smooth. Fold in the meringue.

5. Pour the yogurt mixture into an ice cream maker and freeze according to the manufacturer's directions.

6. Transfer to a freezer-safe container and chill in the freezer for 2 to 3 hours to allow the yogurt to completely set.

Makes 1¼ to 1½ quarts

White Chocolate Raspberry

White chocolate often gets passed over in favor of more intense dark chocolate, but the vanilla and cream flavors of high-quality white chocolate are a great addition to any frozen dessert. This frozen yogurt also includes sweet-tart raspberries, which add their bright color to the dessert and contrast well with the smooth white-chocolate base.

¼ cup water

⅔ cup sugar

2 large egg whites, room temperature

4 ounces white chocolate, melted

2 cups plain Greek-style yogurt, cold

2 teaspoons vanilla extract

¾ cup fresh raspberries

1. Combine the water and sugar in a small saucepan and bring to a boil, without stirring, over medium-high heat. When the sugar mixture comes to a full boil, continue to boil for 1 minute.

2. While the sugar boils, beat the egg whites to soft peaks in a large, clean bowl. When the sugar is ready, continue beating the eggs at low speed and very slowly stream in the hot sugar mixture. When all the sugar has been incorporated, turn the mixer to high and beat until the meringue is glossy and has cooled almost down to room temperature, 2 to 3 minutes. (See The Meringue Method, page 4.)

3. With the mixer on low, blend the melted chocolate into the meringue.

4. Whisk together the yogurt and vanilla in a large bowl until smooth. Fold in the meringue.

5. Pour the yogurt mixture into an ice cream maker and freeze according to the manufacturer's directions.

6. When the yogurt has finished churning and is still soft, transfer to a large bowl. Fold in the fresh raspberries until evenly distributed.

7. Transfer to a freezer-safe container and chill in the freezer for 2 to 3 hours to allow the yogurt to completely set.

Makes 1¼ to 1½ quarts

Peanut Butter

This is a frozen yogurt for peanut-butter lovers, with plenty of peanut-butter flavor packed into every bite. Feel free to use crunchy peanut butter if you're after the texture that the peanut bits will give to the yogurt; otherwise you can opt for the smooth.

- ¼ cup water
- ⅔ cup sugar
- 2 large egg whites, room temperature
- 2 cups plain Greek-style yogurt, cold
- ⅔ cup peanut butter, crunchy or smooth
- ¼ teaspoon salt
- ½ teaspoon vanilla extract

(continued on next page)

1. Combine the water and sugar in a small saucepan and bring to a boil, without stirring, over medium-high heat. When the sugar mixture comes to a full boil, continue to boil for 1 minute.

2. While the sugar boils, beat the egg whites to soft peaks in a large, clean bowl. When the sugar is ready, continue beating the eggs at low speed and very slowly stream in the hot sugar mixture. When all the sugar has been incorporated, turn the mixer to high and beat until the meringue is glossy and has cooled almost down to room temperature, 2 to 3 minutes. (See The Meringue Method, page 4.)

3. Whisk together the yogurt, peanut butter, salt, and vanilla in a large bowl until smooth. Fold in the meringue.

4. Pour the yogurt mixture into an ice cream maker and freeze according to the manufacturer's directions.

5. Transfer to a freezer-safe container and chill in the freezer for 2 to 3 hours to allow the yogurt to completely set.

Makes 1¼ to 1½ quarts

Nutella

Nutella is a delicious and hard-to-resist chocolate-hazelnut spread that is popular worldwide. It's enjoyed as a spread on toast for breakfast and in a wide variety of desserts. A generous dose of Nutella gives this milk chocolate–infused frozen yogurt an extra boost of chocolate and a distinctive nutty flavor instantly recognizable to Nutella fans.

½ cup whole milk

2 ounces milk chocolate, finely chopped

¼ cup water

⅔ cup sugar

2 large egg whites, room temperature

2 cups plain Greek-style yogurt, cold

½ cup Nutella

1 teaspoon vanilla extract

1. Combine the milk and chocolate in a small saucepan and cook over low heat, stirring constantly, until the chocolate is fully incorporated. Set aside to cool to room temperature.

2. Combine the water and sugar in a small saucepan and bring to a boil, without stirring, over medium-high heat. When the sugar mixture comes to a full boil, continue to boil for 1 minute.

3. While the sugar boils, beat the egg whites to soft peaks in a large, clean bowl. When the sugar is ready, continue beating the eggs at low speed and very slowly stream in the hot sugar mixture. When all the sugar has been incorporated, turn the mixer to high and beat until the meringue is glossy and has cooled almost down to room temperature, 2 to 3 minutes. (See The Meringue Method, page 4.)

4. Beat together the yogurt, Nutella, vanilla, and chocolate milk in a large bowl until smooth. Fold in the meringue.

5. Pour the yogurt mixture into an ice cream maker and freeze according to the manufacturer's directions.

6. Transfer to a freezer-safe container and chill in the freezer for 2 to 3 hours to allow the yogurt to completely set.

Makes 1¼ to 1½ quarts

Pistachio

*Pistachios are notable for their color, which is a bit trickier to capture than their subtle flavor. This recipe gives your yogurt a tint of color and bright dots of crunchy chopped nuts, but you can add a few drops of green food coloring to the base if you like. **Note:** Step 1 is simple, but it does need to be done several hours or the day before completing the recipe.*

- ⅔ cup heavy cream
- ⅔ cup raw pistachios, finely chopped
- ¼ cup water
- ⅔ cup sugar
- 2 large egg whites, room temperature
- 2 cups plain Greek-style yogurt, cold
- 1 teaspoon vanilla extract
- ⅔ cup coarsely chopped raw or toasted pistachios

1. Bring the cream to a boil in a small saucepan over medium-high heat. Place the raw pistachios in a small bowl and pour in the hot cream. Cover and allow the pistachios to steep for several hours, or overnight in the refrigerator. Strain the cream into a small bowl and discard the pistachios.

2. Combine the water and sugar in a small saucepan and bring to a boil, without stirring, over medium-high heat. When the sugar mixture comes to a full boil, continue to boil for 1 minute.

3. While the sugar boils, beat the egg whites to soft peaks in a large, clean bowl. When the sugar is ready, continue beating the eggs at low speed and very slowly stream in the hot sugar mixture. When all the sugar has been incorporated, turn the mixer to high and beat until the meringue is glossy and has cooled almost down to room temperature, 2 to 3 minutes. (See The Meringue Method, page 4.)

4. Whisk together the yogurt, vanilla, and pistachio cream in a large bowl until smooth. Fold in the meringue.

5. Pour the yogurt mixture into an ice cream maker and freeze according to the manufacturer's directions.

6. When the yogurt has finished churning and is still soft, transfer to a large bowl. Fold in the coarsely chopped pistachios until evenly distributed.

7. Transfer to a freezer-safe container and chill in the freezer for 2 to 3 hours to allow the yogurt to completely set.

Makes 1¼ to 1½ quarts

Roasted Almond and Amaretto

Amaretto is an almond liqueur with an intense flavor that gives a lot of character to this frozen yogurt. The almond flavor is heightened by the addition of finely chopped toasted almonds, which also give a nice little crunch. Sprinkling the almonds with salt just after toasting lends a hint of savoriness and really brings out their flavor.

1	cup finely chopped unsalted almonds
¼	teaspoon salt
¼	cup water
⅔	cup sugar

(ingredients continued on next page)

2 large egg whites, room temperature

2 cups plain Greek-style yogurt, cold

1 teaspoon vanilla extract

3 tablespoons Amaretto

1. Preheat the oven to 350°F. Spread the almonds on a baking sheet and toast, stirring occasionally, 5 to 10 minutes, until golden. Sprinkle with the salt. Set aside to cool completely.

2. Combine the water and sugar in a small saucepan and bring to a boil, without stirring, over medium-high heat. When the sugar mixture comes to a full boil, continue to boil for 1 minute.

3. While the sugar boils, beat the egg whites to soft peaks in a large, clean bowl. When the sugar is ready, continue beating the eggs at low speed and very slowly stream in the hot sugar mixture. When all the sugar has been incorporated, turn the mixer to high and beat until the meringue is glossy and has cooled almost down to room temperature, 2 to 3 minutes. (See The Meringue Method, page 4.)

4. Whisk together the yogurt, vanilla, and Amaretto in a large bowl until smooth. Fold in the meringue.

5. Pour the yogurt mixture into an ice cream maker and freeze according to the manufacturer's directions.

6. When the yogurt has finished churning and is still soft, transfer to a large bowl. Fold in the toasted almonds until evenly distributed.

7. Transfer to a freezer-safe container and chill in the freezer for 2 to 3 hours to allow the yogurt to completely set.

Makes 1¼ to 1½ quarts

Browned Butter Pecan

The only way to make browned butter even more delicious is by adding pecans to it, and the only way to top that is to make butter pecan frozen yogurt. In this recipe, toasted pecans are coated with browned butter and then added to a nutty, brown butter–infused yogurt for a dessert that gives stiff competition to its ice cream counterpart.

6 tablespoons butter
1 cup finely chopped pecans
¼ cup water
⅔ cup sugar
2 large egg whites, room temperature
2 cups plain Greek-style yogurt, cold
2 teaspoons vanilla extract

1. Place the butter in a small saucepan and melt, without stirring, over medium heat until the butter bubbles and foams, 3 to 4 minutes. When the foam has subsided, it will begin to brown and release a nutty smell. Stir the butter with a spatula as it browns to prevent burning, scraping the brown bits off the bottom of the pan. Cook and stir until the butter is golden brown, 1 to 3 minutes. Transfer to a small bowl and set aside to cool to room temperature.

2. Preheat the oven to 350°F. Spread the pecans on a baking sheet and toast, stirring occasionally, 5 to 10 minutes, until golden. Transfer the pecans to a small bowl and toss with 2 tablespoons of the browned butter. Return the pecans to the baking sheet to cool.

(continued on next page)

3. Combine the water and sugar in a small saucepan and bring to a boil, without stirring, over medium-high heat. When the sugar mixture comes to a full boil, continue to boil for 1 minute.

4. While the sugar boils, beat the egg whites to soft peaks in a large, clean bowl. When the sugar is ready, continue beating the eggs at low speed and very slowly stream in the hot sugar mixture. When all the sugar has been incorporated, turn the mixer to high and beat until the meringue is glossy and has cooled almost down to room temperature, 2 to 3 minutes. (See The Meringue Method, page 4.)

5. Fold the remaining browned butter into about 1 cup of the meringue in a small bowl until incorporated.

6. Whisk together the yogurt and the vanilla in a large bowl until smooth. Fold in the plain meringue and the brown-butter meringue.

7. Pour the yogurt mixture into an ice cream maker and freeze according to the manufacturer's directions.

8. When the yogurt has finished churning and is still soft, transfer to a large bowl. Fold in the buttered pecans until evenly distributed.

9. Transfer to a freezer-safe container and chill in the freezer for 2 to 3 hours to allow the yogurt to completely set.

Makes 1¼ to 1½ quarts

GOURMET

Avocado

The rich creaminess of a perfectly ripe avocado is the very same quality so appealing in ice cream and frozen yogurt, so it's hard to lose when this tropical fruit features in a cold dessert or drink. Here the avocado is paired with honey, the perfect natural sweetener to complement the special character of this fruit.

- 2 large, ripe avocadoes
- ¼ cup water
- ½ cup sugar
- 2 large egg whites, room temperature
- 2 cups plain Greek-style yogurt, cold
- ⅓ cup honey
- 1 teaspoon vanilla extract

(continued on next page)

1. Peel and pit the avocadoes, and then purée in a food processor or mash until very smooth. You should have about 1 cup of avocado purée.

2. Combine the water and sugar in a small saucepan and bring to a boil, without stirring, over medium-high heat. When the sugar mixture comes to a full boil, continue to boil for 1 minute.

3. While the sugar boils, beat the egg whites to soft peaks in a large, clean bowl. When the sugar is ready, continue beating the eggs at low speed and very slowly stream in the hot sugar mixture. When all the sugar has been incorporated, turn the mixer to high and beat until the meringue is glossy and has cooled almost down to room temperature, 2 to 3 minutes. (See The Meringue Method, page 4.)

4. Whisk together the yogurt, avocado purée, honey, and vanilla in a large bowl until smooth. Fold in the meringue.

5. Pour the yogurt mixture into an ice cream maker and freeze according to the manufacturer's directions.

6. Transfer to a freezer-safe container and chill in the freezer for 2 to 3 hours to allow the yogurt to completely set.

Makes 1¼ to 1½ quarts

Maple Bacon

Maple syrup and bacon are terrific at breakfast, and the salty-sweet pair is great in frozen yogurt, too. The cooked bacon is cut into tiny pieces before adding it to the yogurt base to preserve its crispness and add a little crunch.

> 2 ounces bacon
> ¼ cup water
> ½ cup sugar
> 2 large egg whites, room temperature
> 2 cups plain Greek-style yogurt, cold
> ½ teaspoon vanilla extract
> ½ cup maple syrup

1. Cook the bacon in a large skillet over medium heat until completely crisp. Drain on a plate lined with paper towels and cool completely. Chop into very small bits and set aside.

2. Combine the water and sugar in a small saucepan and bring to a boil, without stirring, over medium-high heat. When the sugar mixture comes to a full boil, continue to boil for 1 minute.

3. While the sugar boils, beat the egg whites to soft peaks in a large, clean bowl. When the sugar is ready, continue beating the eggs at low speed and very slowly stream in the hot sugar mixture. When all the sugar has been incorporated, turn the mixer to high and beat until the meringue is glossy and has cooled almost down to room temperature, 2 to 3 minutes. (See The Meringue Method, page 4.)

(continued on next page)

4. Whisk together the yogurt, vanilla, and maple syrup in a large bowl until smooth. Fold in the meringue and the chopped bacon.

5. Pour the yogurt mixture into an ice cream maker and freeze according to the manufacturer's directions.

6. Transfer to a freezer-safe container and chill in the freezer for 2 to 3 hours to allow the yogurt to completely set.

Makes 1¼ to 1½ quarts

Strawberry Cheesecake

The distinctive tang of cream cheese teams up with the tartness of the yogurt in this Strawberry Cheesecake Frozen Yogurt to deliver a taste a lot like real cheesecake! The swirl of graham cracker crumbs brings in the final flavor element and texture of cheesecake. Fresh strawberries add great flavor to this frozen yogurt. Frozen strawberries can be substituted, but be sure to defrost them completely and drain before puréeing.

10–12 ounces fresh strawberries
   ¼ cup water
   ⅔ cup sugar
    2 large egg whites, room temperature
  1½ cups plain Greek-style yogurt, cold
    1 (8-ounce) package cream cheese, at room temperature
    1 teaspoon vanilla extract
   ⅔ cup graham cracker crumbs

1. Wash and hull the strawberries, and then purée in a food processor until very smooth. You should have about 1 cup of strawberry purée.

2. Combine the water and sugar in a small saucepan and bring to a boil, without stirring, over medium-high heat. When the sugar mixture comes to a full boil, continue to boil for 1 minute.

3. While the sugar boils, beat the egg whites to soft peaks in a large, clean bowl. When the sugar is ready, continue beating the eggs at low speed and very slowly stream in the hot sugar mixture. When all the sugar has been incorporated, turn the mixer to high and beat until the meringue is glossy and has cooled almost down to room temperature, 2 to 3 minutes. (See The Meringue Method, page 4.)

4. Beat together the yogurt, cream cheese, vanilla, and strawberry purée in a large bowl or food processor until smooth. If using a food processor, transfer the mixture to a large bowl. Fold in the meringue.

5. Pour the yogurt mixture into an ice cream maker and freeze according to the manufacturer's directions.

6. When the yogurt has finished churning and is still soft, transfer to a large bowl. Swirl in the graham cracker crumbs.

7. Transfer to a freezer-safe container and chill in the freezer for 2 to 3 hours to allow the yogurt to completely set.

Makes 1¼ to 1½ quarts

Vanilla Browned Butter

The rich, nutty flavor of browned butter is even better when it is combined with vanilla, as in this original and truly decadent frozen yogurt.

- ⅓ cup butter
- ¼ cup water
- ⅔ cup sugar
- 1 vanilla bean
- 2 large egg whites, room temperature
- 2 cups plain Greek-style yogurt, cold

1. Place the butter in a small saucepan and melt over medium heat until the butter bubbles and foams, 3 to 4 minutes. When the foam has subsided, it will begin to brown and release a nutty smell. Stir the butter with a spatula as it browns to prevent burning, scraping the brown bits off the bottom of the pan. Cook and stir until the butter is golden brown, 1 to 3 minutes. Transfer to a small bowl and set aside to cool to room temperature.

2. Combine the water and sugar in a small saucepan. Split the vanilla bean lengthwise and scrape the seeds out using the back of a knife. Add the seeds to the sugar mixture. Bring to a boil, without stirring, over medium-high heat. When the sugar mixture comes to a full boil, continue to boil for 1 minute.

3. While the sugar boils, beat the egg whites to soft peaks in a large, clean bowl. When the sugar is ready, continue beating the eggs at low speed and very slowly stream in the hot sugar mixture. When all the sugar has been incorporated, turn the

mixer to high and beat until the meringue is glossy and has cooled almost down to room temperature, 2 to 3 minutes. (See The Meringue Method, page 4.)

4. Whisk together the yogurt and browned butter in a large bowl until smooth. Fold in the meringue.

5. Pour the yogurt mixture into an ice cream maker and freeze according to the manufacturer's directions.

6. Transfer to a freezer-safe container and chill in the freezer for 2 to 3 hours to allow the yogurt to completely set.

Makes 1¼ to 1½ quarts

Creamsicle

The special appeal of a Creamsicle is the vanilla cream filling surrounded by the zesty coating of orange. To get those flavors and textures into frozen yogurt, this version is flavored with a whole vanilla bean, orange zest, and orange oil, an intensely flavored extract of the same oil found in orange zest. The result is smooth, creamy, and clearly inspired by the frozen treat on a stick.

- ¼ cup water
- ⅔ cup sugar
- 1 vanilla bean
- 2 large egg whites, room temperature
- 2 cups plain Greek-style yogurt, cold
- 1½ tablespoons orange zest
- ½ teaspoon orange oil

(continued on next page)

1. Combine the water and sugar in a small saucepan. Split the vanilla bean lengthwise and scrape the seeds out using the back of a knife. Add the seeds to the sugar mixture. Bring to a boil, without stirring, over medium-high heat. When the sugar mixture comes to a full boil, continue to boil for 1 minute.

2. While the sugar boils, beat the egg whites to soft peaks in a large, clean bowl. When the sugar is ready, continue beating the eggs at low speed and very slowly stream in the hot sugar mixture. When all the sugar has been incorporated, turn the mixer to high and beat until the meringue is glossy and has cooled almost down to room temperature, 2 to 3 minutes. (See The Meringue Method, page 4.)

3. Whisk together the yogurt, orange zest, and orange oil in a large bowl until smooth. Fold in the meringue.

4. Pour the yogurt mixture into an ice cream maker and freeze according to the manufacturer's directions.

5. Transfer to a freezer-safe container and chill in the freezer for 2 to 3 hours to allow the yogurt to completely set.

Makes 1¼ to 1½ quarts

Elvis

It's on record that Elvis's favorite sandwich was peanut butter, banana, and honey. Delicious in a hot, toasted sandwich, those same ingredients in this frozen version produce a creamy, savory-sweet sensation in every spoonful that's sure to win over many fans.

- 1 large ripe banana
- ¼ cup water
- ½ cup sugar
- 2 large egg whites, room temperature
- 2 cups plain Greek-style yogurt, cold
- ⅔ cup crunchy or smooth peanut butter
- ⅓ cup honey
- ¼ teaspoon salt
- ½ teaspoon vanilla extract

1. Cut the banana into small pieces. Spread in an even layer on a plate or baking dish and place in the freezer to chill.

2. Combine the water and sugar in a small saucepan and bring to a boil, without stirring, over medium-high heat. When the sugar mixture comes to a full boil, continue to boil for 1 minute.

3. While the sugar boils, beat the egg whites to soft peaks in a large, clean bowl. When the sugar is ready, continue beating the eggs at low speed and very slowly stream in the hot sugar mixture. When all the sugar has been incorporated, turn the mixer to high and beat until the meringue is glossy and has cooled almost down to room temperature, 2 to 3 minutes. (See The Meringue Method, page 4.)

(continued on next page)

4. Beat together the yogurt, peanut butter, honey, salt, and vanilla in a large bowl until smooth. Fold in the meringue.

5. Pour the yogurt mixture into an ice cream maker and freeze according to the manufacturer's directions.

6. When the yogurt has finished churning and is still soft, transfer to a large bowl. Fold in the chilled banana pieces until evenly distributed.

7. Transfer to a freezer-safe container and chill in the freezer for 2 to 3 hours to allow the yogurt to completely set.

Makes 1¼ to 1½ quarts

Mexican Spiced Hot Chocolate

Mexican table chocolate is a coarse, dark chocolate flavored with spices that often include cinnamon and cayenne, which give a little heat to the chocolate. It's sold in blocks and commonly used to make a spicy — and addictive — hot drink. Those flavors also make a spicy and addictive frozen yogurt.

- ½ cup whole milk
- 2 ounces Mexican table chocolate or dark chocolate, finely chopped
- 2 tablespoons unsweetened cocoa powder
- ¾ teaspoon ground cinnamon
- ½ teaspoon ground cayenne pepper
- ¼ cup water
- ⅔ cup sugar

2 large egg whites, room temperature
2 cups plain Greek-style yogurt, cold
1 teaspoon vanilla extract
¼ teaspoon almond extract

1. Bring the milk to a simmer in a small saucepan. Combine the chocolate, cocoa, cinnamon, and cayenne in a small bowl and pour in the hot milk. Stir to dissolve. Set aside to cool to room temperature.

2. Combine the water and sugar in a small saucepan and bring to a boil, without stirring, over medium-high heat. When the sugar mixture comes to a full boil, continue to boil for 1 minute.

3. While the sugar boils, beat the egg whites to soft peaks in a large, clean bowl. When the sugar is ready, continue beating the eggs at low speed and very slowly stream in the hot sugar mixture. When all the sugar has been incorporated, turn the mixer to high and beat until the meringue is glossy and has cooled almost down to room temperature, 2 to 3 minutes. (See The Meringue Method, page 4.)

4. Whisk together the yogurt, vanilla, almond extract, and chocolate mixture in a large bowl until smooth. Fold in the meringue.

5. Pour the yogurt mixture into an ice cream maker and freeze according to the manufacturer's directions.

6. Transfer to a freezer-safe container and chill in the freezer for 2 to 3 hours to allow the yogurt to completely set.

Makes 1¼ to 1½ quarts

Dulce de Leche

Dulce de leche is a thick, milky caramel sauce that is made by caramelizing sweetened condensed milk. Its rich flavor is decadent and it is a popular ingredient in many Latin American desserts. The caramel sauce is scrumptious in frozen yogurt, too.

¼ cup water

½ cup sugar

2 large egg whites, room temperature

2 cups plain Greek-style yogurt, cold

½ cup Dulce de Leche, homemade or store bought (recipe follows)

1 teaspoon vanilla extract

¼ teaspoon salt

1. Combine the water and sugar in a small saucepan and bring to a boil, without stirring, over medium-high heat. When the sugar mixture comes to a full boil, continue to boil for 1 minute.

2. While the sugar boils, beat the egg whites to soft peaks in a large, clean bowl. When the sugar is ready, continue beating the eggs at low speed and very slowly stream in the hot sugar mixture. When all the sugar has been incorporated, turn the mixer to high and beat until the meringue is glossy and has cooled almost down to room temperature, 2 to 3 minutes. (See The Meringue Method, page 4.)

3. Beat together the yogurt, dulce de leche, vanilla, and salt in a large bowl until smooth. Fold in the meringue.

4. Pour the yogurt mixture into an ice cream maker and freeze according to the manufacturer's directions.

5. Transfer to a freezer-safe container and chill in the freezer for 2 to 3 hours to allow the yogurt to completely set.

Makes 1¼ to 1½ quarts

Dulce de Leche

1 (14-ounce) can sweetened condensed milk

1. Pour the milk into a heatproof bowl set over a pan of briskly simmering water, a setup known as a double boiler. Cook, stirring occasionally to maintain a smooth consistency, until the milk is thick and deep golden, 60 to 70 minutes. Be careful not to let all the water cook off; if the water level in the pan becomes too low, replenish with additional hot water.

2. Remove the bowl from the heat and cool completely before using. The dulce de leche can be made 1 to 2 days in advance and stored in an airtight container at room temperature.

Makes about 1 cup

Honey and Goat Cheese

Goat cheese, much like cream cheese, is a soft cheese that adds a particular flavor and texture to many desserts. This frozen yogurt brings together honey and goat cheese, but the cheese also works extremely well with berries, and a delicious variation on this basic recipe would be to fold in fresh raspberries or blueberries after churning.

　¼　cup water
　½　cup sugar
　2　large egg whites, room temperature
　2　cups plain Greek-style yogurt, cold
　⅓　cup goat cheese, softened
　⅓　cup honey
　2　teaspoons vanilla extract

1. Combine the water and sugar in a small saucepan and bring to a boil, without stirring, over medium-high heat. When the sugar mixture comes to a full boil, continue to boil for 1 minute.

2. While the sugar boils, beat the egg whites to soft peaks in a large, clean bowl. When the sugar is ready, continue beating the eggs at low speed and very slowly stream in the hot sugar mixture. When all the sugar has been incorporated, turn the mixer to high and beat until the meringue is glossy and has cooled almost down to room temperature, 2 to 3 minutes. (See The Meringue Method, page 4.)

3. Beat together the yogurt, cheese, honey, and vanilla in a large bowl or food processor until smooth. If using a food processor, transfer the mixture to a large bowl. Fold in the meringue.

4. Pour the yogurt mixture into an ice cream maker and freeze according to the manufacturer's directions.

5. Transfer to a freezer-safe container and chill in the freezer for 2 to 3 hours to allow the yogurt to completely set.

Makes 1¼ to 1½ quarts

Bananas Foster

A popular dessert in the 1950s, bananas Foster was often seen at fine dining restaurants around the country. It is made by cooking bananas in brown sugar and butter, then flambéing the mixture with a splash of dark rum. This modern frozen yogurt version doesn't pack the same flash as a flambé pan, but it captures perfectly those same great flavors.

- 3 tablespoons butter
- ⅓ cup firmly packed brown sugar
- ¾ cup mashed banana (from 2 ripe bananas)
- ¼ cup dark rum
- ¼ cup water
- ½ cup granulated sugar
- 2 large egg whites, room temperature
- 2 cups plain Greek-style yogurt, cold

1. Melt together the butter and brown sugar in a small saucepan or skillet over low heat. Cook, stirring, until the brown sugar has dissolved. Add the mashed banana and cook, stirring, until the mixture begins to caramelize and thicken slightly, 3 to 4 minutes. Remove from the heat and stir in the rum. Set aside.

(continued on next page)

2. Combine the water and granulated sugar in a small saucepan and bring to a boil, without stirring, over medium-high heat. When the sugar mixture comes to a full boil, continue to boil for 1 minute.

3. While the sugar boils, beat the egg whites to soft peaks in a large, clean bowl. When the sugar is ready, continue beating the eggs at low speed and very slowly stream in the hot sugar mixture. When all the sugar has been incorporated, turn the mixer to high and beat until the meringue is glossy and has cooled almost down to room temperature, 2 to 3 minutes. (See The Meringue Method, page 4.)

4. Whisk together the yogurt and the banana mixture in a large bowl until smooth. Fold in the meringue.

5. Pour the yogurt mixture into an ice cream maker and freeze according to the manufacturer's directions.

6. Transfer to a freezer-safe container and chill in the freezer for 2 to 3 hours to allow the yogurt to completely set.

Makes 1¼ to 1½ quarts

Peach Melba

Peach melba is a classic dessert that combines peaches and raspberries with ice cream. It was invented at the end of the nineteenth century, and though the dessert may not seem quite as exotic as it did when ice cream and frozen desserts were still a novelty, this flavor combination never goes out of style.

   3 large peaches (about 1 pound)
  ¼ cup water

⅔ cup sugar

2 large egg whites, room temperature

2 cups plain Greek-style yogurt, cold

2 teaspoons vanilla extract

½ cup Raspberry Coulis (recipe follows), plus more for serving

1. Peel and pit the peaches, and then purée in a food processor until very smooth. You should have about 1 cup of peach purée.

2. Combine the water and sugar in a small saucepan and bring to a boil, without stirring, over medium-high heat. When the sugar mixture comes to a full boil, continue to boil for 1 minute.

3. While the sugar boils, beat the egg whites to soft peaks in a large, clean bowl. When the sugar is ready, continue beating the eggs at low speed and very slowly stream in the hot sugar mixture. When all the sugar has been incorporated, turn the mixer to high and beat until the meringue is glossy and has cooled almost down to room temperature, 2 to 3 minutes. (See The Meringue Method, page 4.)

4. Whisk together the yogurt, peach purée, and vanilla in a large bowl until smooth. Fold in the meringue.

5. Pour the yogurt mixture into an ice cream maker and freeze according to the manufacturer's directions.

6. When the yogurt has finished churning and is still soft, transfer to a large bowl. Swirl in ½ cup of the raspberry coulis.

7. Transfer to a freezer-safe container and chill in the freezer for 2 to 3 hours to allow the yogurt to completely set.

(continued on next page)

8. Drizzle each serving with 1 to 2 tablespoons of the remaining coulis.

Makes 1¼ to 1½ quarts

Raspberry Coulis

- ½ cup sugar
- 12 ounces fresh raspberries
- ¼ cup water

1. Combine the sugar, berries, and water in a medium saucepan and bring to a boil over medium-high heat. Reduce the heat to medium and cook until the fruit begins to break down and the sauce thickens, about 5 minutes. Remove from the heat and allow to cool.

2. Pour the mixture into a fine sieve over a small bowl and press, using the back of a wooden spoon. Discard the solids. Store in an airtight container in the refrigerator for up to 1 week.

Makes about 1 cup

Mint Julep

The mint julep cocktail is the traditional drink served at the running of the Kentucky Derby every year. It combines mint, bourbon, and vanilla for a flavor that is surprisingly refreshing and very grown-up.

- ¼ cup water
- ½ cup sugar

2 large egg whites, room temperature

2 cups plain Greek-style yogurt, cold

¼ cup bourbon

1 teaspoon vanilla extract

1 teaspoon peppermint extract

1. Combine the water and sugar in a small saucepan and bring to a boil, without stirring, over medium-high heat. When the sugar mixture comes to a full boil, continue to boil for 1 minute.

2. While the sugar boils, beat the egg whites to soft peaks in a large, clean bowl. When the sugar is ready, continue beating the eggs at low speed and very slowly stream in the hot sugar mixture. When all the sugar has been incorporated, turn the mixer to high and beat until the meringue is glossy and has cooled down to almost room temperature, 2 to 3 minutes. (See The Meringue Method, page 4.)

3. Whisk together the yogurt, bourbon, vanilla, and peppermint extract in a large bowl until smooth. Fold in the meringue.

4. Pour the yogurt mixture into an ice cream maker and freeze according to the manufacturer's directions.

5. Transfer to a freezer-safe container and chill in the freezer for 2 to 3 hours to allow the yogurt to completely set.

Makes 1¼ to 1½ quarts

Grasshopper

The grasshopper cocktail first became popular in the 1950s and 1960s as an after-dinner drink. It features crème de cacao and crème de menthe, which give it the refreshing chocolate-mint flavor and distinctive bright green color for which it's known. You'll find those same great flavors in the frozen yogurt, but you might want to give it a little boost of food coloring to capture the cocktail's signature green hue.

- ¼ cup water
- ⅔ cup sugar
- 2 large egg whites, room temperature
- 2 cups plain Greek-style yogurt, cold
- 2 tablespoons crème de cacao
- 2 tablespoons crème de menthe
- ½ teaspoon peppermint extract
- ½ teaspoon green food coloring (optional)

1. Combine the water and sugar in a small saucepan and bring to a boil, without stirring, over medium-high heat. When the sugar mixture comes to a full boil, continue to boil for 1 minute.

2. While the sugar boils, beat the egg whites to soft peaks in a large, clean bowl. When the sugar is ready, continue beating the eggs at low speed and very slowly stream in the hot sugar mixture. When all the sugar has been incorporated, turn the mixer to high and beat until the meringue is glossy and has cooled almost down to room temperature, 2 to 3 minutes. (See The Meringue Method, page 4.)

3. Whisk together the yogurt, crème de cacao, crème de menthe, and peppermint extract in a large bowl until smooth. Whisk in the food coloring, if using. Fold in the meringue.

4. Pour the yogurt mixture into an ice cream maker and freeze according to the manufacturer's directions.

5. Transfer to a freezer-safe container and chill in the freezer for 2 to 3 hours to allow the yogurt to completely set.

Makes 1¼ to 1½ quarts

HOLIDAY

Candy Cane

Candy canes are instantly recognizable, and this peppermint frozen yogurt sports the same swirled look with the help of a little food coloring. The optional splash of peppermint schnapps boosts the peppermint flavor in this dessert and makes it a little more grown-up, and bits of chopped peppermint or candy cane offer a nice crunch.

- ¼ cup water
- ⅔ cup sugar
- 2 large egg whites, room temperature
- 2 cups plain Greek-style yogurt, cold
- 1 teaspoon vanilla extract
- 1 teaspoon peppermint extract
- 2 tablespoons peppermint schnapps (optional)
- ½ cup crushed peppermint candies or candy canes
- ¼ teaspoon red food coloring

1. Combine the water and sugar in a small saucepan and bring to a boil, without stirring, over medium-high heat. When the sugar mixture comes to a full boil, continue to boil for 1 minute.

2. While the sugar boils, beat the egg whites to soft peaks in a large, clean bowl. When the sugar is ready, continue beating the eggs at low speed and very slowly stream in the hot sugar mixture. When all the sugar has been incorporated, turn the mixer to high and beat until the meringue is glossy and has cooled almost down to room temperature, 2 to 3 minutes. (See The Meringue Method, page 4.)

3. Whisk together the yogurt, vanilla and peppermint extracts, and the schnapps, if using, in a large bowl until smooth. Fold in the meringue.

4. Pour the yogurt mixture into an ice cream maker and freeze according to the manufacturer's directions.

5. When the yogurt has finished churning and is still soft, transfer to a large bowl. Set aside ½ cup in a small bowl. Fold the crushed peppermint into the yogurt in the large bowl. Stir the food coloring into the yogurt in the small bowl until well incorporated. Fold the red-tinted yogurt into the yogurt in the large bowl to create a swirled effect.

6. Transfer to a freezer-safe container and chill in the freezer for 2 to 3 hours to allow the yogurt to completely set.

Makes 1¼ to 1½ quarts

Spiced Pumpkin Pie

Pumpkin pie is synonymous with the fall holidays. Often served with whipped cream or ice cream, here it's in a frozen dessert. The small amount of cooked pumpkin filling captures the flavors of the popular pie and incorporates easily into the frozen yogurt. Even frozen, it doesn't mind a generous topping of whipped cream.

1 cup pumpkin purée, canned is fine

⅓ cup firmly packed brown sugar

¼ cup whole milk

1 teaspoon ground cinnamon

½ teaspoon ground ginger

¼ teaspoon ground cloves

¼ teaspoon ground nutmeg

1 teaspoon vanilla extract

¼ cup water

½ cup granulated sugar

2 large egg whites, room temperature

2 cups plain Greek-style yogurt, cold

1. Whisk together the pumpkin, brown sugar, milk, cinnamon, ginger, cloves, nutmeg, and vanilla in a medium saucepan. Cook, stirring constantly, over medium heat until the sugar has dissolved. Set aside to cool to room temperature.

2. Combine the water and granulated sugar in a small saucepan and bring to a boil, without stirring, over medium-high heat. When the sugar mixture comes to a full boil, continue to boil for 1 minute.

3. While the sugar boils, beat the egg whites to soft peaks in a large, clean bowl. When the sugar is ready, continue beating the eggs at low speed and very slowly stream in the hot sugar mixture. When all the sugar has been incorporated, turn the mixer to high and beat until the meringue is glossy and has cooled almost down to room temperature, 2 to 3 minutes. (See The Meringue Method, page 4.)

4. Whisk together the yogurt and the pumpkin mixture in a large bowl until smooth. Fold in the meringue.

5. Pour the yogurt mixture into an ice cream maker and freeze according to the manufacturer's directions.

6. Transfer to a freezer-safe container and chill in the freezer for 2 to 3 hours to allow the yogurt to completely set.

Makes 1¼ to 1½ quarts

Cranberry

Ruby red and sweet-tart, cranberries are popular in both side dishes and desserts around the holidays. This recipe adds to the lineup not only the tang of the yogurt, but also a dash of almond.

 ¼ cup water
 ½ cup sugar
 2 large egg whites, room temperature
 2 cups plain Greek-style yogurt, cold
 1 cup Cranberry Sauce (recipe follows)
 1 teaspoon vanilla extract
 ¼ teaspoon almond extract

(continued on next page)

1. Combine the water and sugar in a small saucepan and bring to a boil, without stirring, over medium-high heat. When the sugar mixture comes to a full boil, continue to boil for 1 minute.

2. While the sugar boils, beat the egg whites to soft peaks in a large, clean bowl. When the sugar is ready, continue beating the eggs at low speed and very slowly stream in the hot sugar mixture. When all the sugar has been incorporated, turn the mixer to high and beat until the meringue is glossy and has cooled almost down to room temperature, 2 to 3 minutes. (See The Meringue Method, page 4.)

3. Whisk together the yogurt, cranberry sauce, vanilla, and almond extract in a large bowl until smooth. Fold in the meringue.

4. Pour the yogurt mixture into an ice cream maker and freeze according to the manufacturer's directions.

Makes 1¼ to 1½ quarts

Cranberry Sauce

   8 ounces fresh or frozen cranberries
   ⅓ cup water
   ¾ cup brown sugar, firmly packed
   ¼ teaspoon ground allspice

1. Combine the cranberries and water in a medium saucepan. Cook over medium-high heat until the cranberries begin to pop, 3 to 4 minutes.

2. Add the brown sugar and allspice and continue cooking, stirring occasionally, until the sugar has dissolved and the mixture comes to a full boil. Boil, stirring occasionally, until the mixture thickens slightly, 3 to 4 minutes. Remove from the heat and set aside to cool to room temperature. The sauce can be stored in an airtight container in the refrigerator for up to 1 week.

Makes about 1 cup

Eggnog

Thick, rich eggnog, perfumed by nutmeg and vanilla, is a holiday staple, and this frozen version is a cool way to enjoy it. Freshly grated nutmeg and vanilla make the eggnog pop, and the splash of bourbon or dark rum supplies the same warming kick as the classic drink. If preferred, you can substitute rum extract for the alcohol.

- ¼ cup water
- ⅔ cup sugar
- 2 large egg whites, room temperature
- 2 cups plain Greek-style yogurt, cold
- 1 cup eggnog
- ½ teaspoon freshly grated nutmeg
- 2 teaspoons vanilla extract
- 2 tablespoons bourbon or dark rum (optional)

1. Combine the water and sugar in a small saucepan and bring to a boil, without stirring, over medium-high heat. When the sugar mixture comes to a full boil, continue to boil for 1 minute.

(continued on next page)

2. While the sugar boils, beat the egg whites to soft peaks in a large, clean bowl. When the sugar is ready, continue beating the eggs at low speed and very slowly stream in the hot sugar mixture. When all the sugar has been incorporated, turn the mixer to high and beat until the meringue is glossy and has cooled almost down to room temperature, 2 to 3 minutes. (See The Meringue Method, page 4.)

3. Whisk together the yogurt, eggnog, nutmeg, vanilla, and bourbon, if using, in a large bowl until smooth. Fold in the meringue.

4. Pour the yogurt mixture into an ice cream maker and freeze according to the manufacturer's directions.

5. Transfer to a freezer-safe container and chill in the freezer for 2 to 3 hours to allow the yogurt to completely set.

Makes 1¼ to 1½ quarts

Gingerbread

Sweet, spicy gingerbread is another confection that evokes the holidays. Most gingerbreads include molasses, brown sugar, ginger, and cinnamon. This version calls for a pinch of black pepper to make the other spices come through a little bit more. For even more spice, toss in some finely chopped candied ginger after churning. Good on its own, this frozen yogurt is also especially good served with a piece of gingerbread or spice cake, slightly warmed.

½ cup whole milk

¼ cup unsulphured molasses

⅓ cup firmly packed brown sugar

2 tablespoons grated fresh ginger

1 teaspoon ground cinnamon

¼ teaspoon black pepper

¼ cup water

½ cup granulated sugar

2 large egg whites, room temperature

2 cups plain Greek-style yogurt, cold

1 teaspoon vanilla extract

⅓ cup candied ginger, finely chopped (optional)

1. Bring the milk, molasses, brown sugar, ginger, cinnamon, and pepper to a simmer in a small saucepan over medium heat. Cook, stirring, until the sugar has dissolved. When the mixture comes to a boil, remove from the heat and allow to cool to room temperature.

2. Strain the milk mixture into a small bowl and set aside.

(continued on next page)

3. Combine the water and sugar in a small saucepan and bring to a boil, without stirring, over medium-high heat. When the sugar mixture comes to a full boil, continue to boil for 1 minute.

4. While the sugar boils, beat the egg whites to soft peaks in a large, clean bowl. When the sugar is ready, continue beating the eggs at low speed and very slowly stream in the hot sugar mixture. When all the sugar has been incorporated, turn the mixer to high and beat until the meringue is glossy and has cooled almost down to room temperature, 2 to 3 minutes. (See The Meringue Method, page 4.)

5. Whisk together the yogurt, vanilla, and spiced milk in a large bowl until smooth. Fold in the meringue.

6. Pour the yogurt mixture into an ice cream maker and freeze according to the manufacturer's directions.

7. When the yogurt has finished churning and is still soft, transfer to a large bowl. Fold in the candied ginger, if using, until evenly distributed.

8. Transfer to a freezer-safe container and chill in the freezer for 2 to 3 hours to allow the yogurt to completely set.

Makes 1¼ to 1½ quarts

Metric Conversion Chart

Unless you have finely calibrated measuring equipment, conversions between U.S. and metric measurements will be somewhat inexact. It's important to convert the measurements for all of the ingredients in a recipe to maintain the same proportions as the original.

General Formula for Metric Conversion	
Ounces to grams	multiply ounces by 28.35
Grams to ounces	multiply grams by 0.035
Pounds to grams	multiply pounds by 453.5
Pounds to kilograms	multiply pounds by 0.45
Cups to liters	multiply cups by 0.24
Fahrenheit to Celsius	subtract 32 from Fahrenheit temperature, multiply by 5, then divide by 9
Celsius to Fahrenheit	multiply Celsius temperature by 9, divide by 5, then add 32

Approximate Equivalent by Volume			
U.S.	METRIC	U.S.	METRIC
1 teaspoon	5 milliliters	2 cups	460 milliliters
1 tablespoon	15 milliliters	4 cups (1 quart)	0.95 liter
½ cup	120 milliliters	1.06 quarts	1 liter
1 cup	230 milliliters		

Approximate Equivalent by Weight			
U.S.	METRIC	METRIC	U.S.
½ ounce	14 grams	1 gram	0.035 ounce
1 ounce	28 grams	50 grams	1.75 ounces
1½ ounces	40 grams	100 grams	3.5 ounces
2½ ounces	70 grams	250 grams	8.75 ounces
4 ounces	112 grams	500 grams	1.1 pounds
8 ounces	228 grams	1 kilogram	2.2 pounds
16 ounces (1 pound)	454 grams		

OTHER STOREY TITLES YOU WILL ENJOY

The Beginner's Guide to Preserving Food at Home
by Janet Chadwick
The best and quickest methods for preserving every common vegetable
and fruit, with easy instructions to encourage even first-timers.
240 pages. Paper. ISBN 978-1-60342-145-4.

The Donut Book by Sally Levitt Steinberg
A deliciously engaging book that explores the nostalgia
and history of the donut.
192 pages. Paper. ISBN 978-1-58017-548-7.

Homemade Liqueurs and Infused Spirits by Andrew Schloss
Over 130 intriguing and original flavor combinations and 21 clone recipes
for big-name brand liqueurs.
272 pages. Paper. ISBN 978-1-61212-098-0.

Homemade Soda by Andrew Schloss
Recipes for a spectacular variety of fizzy juices, sparkling waters, root
beers, colas, and other carbonated concoctions.
336 pages. Paper. ISBN 978-1-60342-796-8.

Hot Sauce! by Jennifer Trainer Thompson
More than 30 recipes to make your own, plus 60 more recipes
for cooking with homemade or commercial sauces.
192 pages. Paper. ISBN 978-1-60342-816-3.

These and other books from Storey Publishing are available
wherever quality books are sold or by calling 1-800-441-5700.
Visit us at *www.storey.com* or sign up for our newsletter
at *www.storey.com/signup*.